500

MR. WILLIAM JAROSZEWSKI
2123 West Roger St.
South Bend, Indiana 46628

HISTORY OF BROADCASTING: RADIO TO TELEVISION

HISTORY OF BROADCASTING: Radio to Television

Radio Today

ARNO HUTH

ARNO PRESS and THE NEW YORK TIMES

New York • 1971

Reprint Edition 1971 by Arno Press Inc.

Reprinted from a copy in The University of Illinois Library

LC# 77-161179
ISBN 0-405-03585-3

HISTORY OF BROADCASTING: RADIO TO TELEVISION
ISBN for complete set: 0-405-03555-1
See last pages of this volume for titles.

Manufactured in the United States of America

GENEVA RESEARCH CENTRE

RADIO TODAY

THE PRESENT STATE OF BROADCASTING

BY

ARNO HUTH

GENEVA STUDIES, VOL. XII. No. 6   JULY, 1942

TO THE MEMORY
OF GUGLIELMO MARCONI

EDITORIAL NOTE

———

Dr. Arno Huth, the author of the present study, is well-known in the international radio world. His publications, in French as well as in English, have attracted attention in many quarters. The present study, which was drafted for the *Geneva Studies* in French, has been translated into English by Miss Hélène Héroys.

The generosity of the Rockefeller Foundation has allowed the Graduate Institute of International Studies to undertake the completion of the programme of studies initiated by the Geneva Research Centre. We are very glad to be able to publish this monograph in the series of the *Geneva Studies*. In doing so, we need hardly recall that, as the Centre, this Institute pursues no international policy of its own and is in no way responsible for the opinions expressed in studies published under its auspices.

William E. Rappard.

———

ABBREVIATIONS

ABC	=	Australian Broadcasting Commission, Sydney
AVRO	=	Algemeene Vereeniging Radio Omroep, Amsterdam
AWA	=	Amalgamated Wireless Australasia, Ltd., Sydney
BBC	=	British Broadcasting Corporation, London
Bulletin IBU	=	*Monthly Bulletin of the International Broadcasting Union*, Geneva (English edition of the *Bulletin mensuel de l'Union Internationale de Radiodiffusion*).
CBC	=	Canadian Broadcasting Corporation, Ottawa
CBS	=	Columbia Broadcasting System, New York
EIAR	=	Ente Italiano per le Audizioni Radiofoniche, Rome
FCC	=	Federal Communications Commission, Washington D.C.
FM	=	Frequency Modulation Broadcasting
IBU	=	International Broadcasting Union, Geneva
kc	=	kilocycles per second
kW	=	kilowatt (1000 watts)
kWh	=	kilowatt-hour
MBS	=	Mutual Broadcasting System, New York
NAB	=	National Association of Broadcasters, Washington D.C.
NBC	=	National Broadcasting Company, New York
PHOHI	=	N.V. Philip's Omroep Holland-Indië, Eindhoven
RCA	=	Radio Corporation of America, New York
RRG	=	Reichs-Rundfunk-Gesellschaft m.b.H., Berlin
SABC	=	South African Broadcasting Corporation, Johannesburg
SODRE	=	Servicio Oficial de Difusión Radio Electrica, Montevideo

TABLE OF CONTENTS

PREFACE

The radio is a "ship which sails at tremendous speed" wrote the late Senator Guglielmo Marconi in his foreword to the author's first book on broadcasting [1]. Considering the rapidity of radio development, he expressed the hope that this work, in which he saw the record of a "stage" reached by broadcasting, would soon be followed by the record of another "stage". Five years have elapsed since then and, though the author has been able to study many special questions in this field, circumstances have prevented him from publishing a new edition of this somewhat encyclopædic book. Similarly, they have delayed the completion of an extensive study on International Broadcasting, started a year ago under the auspices of the Geneva Research Centre. He would like however to answer the wish of Marconi in the following pages, dedicated to the memory of this great pioneer of the radio.

It is of course impossible, within the framework of a short study, to treat exhaustively all the questions involved or to analyze the activities of the radio in all their aspects. The author hopes nevertheless that he may have succeeded in giving—on the basis of authoritative documents and research— a general view of the present state of radio broadcasting and of the fundamental changes which have taken place lately.

The situation of broadcasting has been upset in many regions. Stations have been destroyed, others have changed owners, and many services have been suppressed or reorganized according to principles entirely different from their former status. Programmes have been greatly influenced by political events and new tasks have been assigned to the radio in the service of propaganda and national defence. But the development of radio broadcasting has not stopped ; although in a few countries, progress seems to be at a standstill, in the others this development continues normally or has even been

---

[1] *La Radiodiffusion, Puissance Mondiale* (Radio Broadcasting — A World Power), Paris 1937.

accelerated under the influence of present events and the interest they arouse. On the other hand, any war time decision is likely to be altered in peace time and has therefore merely a provisional character.

Consequently, this study does not aim at describing "wartime broadcasting". While mentioning the changes which have occurred at the beginning and in the course of the present war, the author would rather stress those permanent factors which are determinant in broadcasting—such as the problems which broadcasters have to face, the solutions that have been adopted, the organization of services, the composition of programmes, the methods of reception and the audience, and finally, the recent technical developments.

The author would be very grateful to his readers if they would kindly call his attention to any errors he may have made —these are always possible in such matters, especially in the present circumstances—or communicate to him any new information which might to be of importance for his future studies and publications.

The author wishes here to express his gratitude to Professor Pitman B. Potter who has always shown great interest in his work, and to Professor William E. Rappard who has entrusted him with the writing of this study. His thanks must also go to the Directors and officers of the Bureau of the International Telecommunications Union, Berne, and the Office of the International Broadcasting Union, Geneva, who have greatly facilitated his research, and also to Mr. John H. Payne, Chief of the Electrical Division of the U.S. Department of Commerce, Dr. Max Jordan, European Director of the National Broadcasting Company, Mr. Martin Codel, publisher of the American magazine *Broadcasting*, and Señor Adolfo T. Cosentino, Chief of the Argentine Direction of Radiocommunications, to whom he owes much interesting information.

Lastly, it would be unfair not to pay a tribute to the extremely valuable collaboration of my wife, who has taken an active share in this work.

A. H.

Geneva, March 1942.

INTRODUCTION

Fifty-five years ago Heinrich Hertz discovered the electric waves. Forty-seven years ago Marconi applied them to the transmission of messages. In 1899 the first radiogram crossed the Channel and two years later the signals crossed the Atlantic.

Wireless telegraphy was followed by wireless telephony and, after the war, by radio broadcasting. It is strange to realize that only twenty years have passed since that "heroic epoch" when a few awestruck men took possession of this new kingdom.

No invention of our time has had a greater development and influence, none has conquered the world in so short a time. Taken first for a curious toy, for a simple entertainment, broadcasting soon proved to be a vital force, affecting the political, social, and economic spheres as well as the cultural, educational, and religious.

Today broadcasting is a world power—a power which has a vast and complex organization, an army of collaborators, big financial and other resources, and which wields tremendous influence in the furthermost quarters of the globe.

In order to estimate this power it is essential to appreciate the part played by broadcasting in our time, to make a close study of its foundations and its structure, its means and its activities, and also its position in the various countries and continents.

A. THE STRUCTURE OF BROADCASTING

I. ORGANIZATION AND FINANCING

The development of broadcasting was so rapid and so sudden that it was impossible to consider the building in advance of the foundations on which this gigantic edifice must rest.

The men who—in 1920 in America, in 1921 in Europe—created the first stations and sent out the first transmissions, were not "broadcasters" but rather technicians and bold amateurs, small groups of listeners, scientific bodies or else radio manufacturers. For some, broadcasting was above all a field of research, for others an original means of advertising. They lacked the time and inclination to concern themselves with the innumerable questions that were involved in radio or to medidate on its tasks and its future mission.

It is only after years of experimenting and of errors dearly paid for, it is only under the threat of chaos in the air and thanks to a better understanding of the heavy responsibility resulting from the possibilities of broadcasting, that an effort was at last made to solve these new problems, of which the most important and the most urgent was that of organization.

Starting from private initiative, broadcasting could not escape the control of the state. First, certain of its characteristics necessitated from their very nature legislative measures: universal propagation of the waves, ignorant of national frontiers ; the limited number of available frequencies, requiring a distribution of wave-lengths amongst all those interested; the danger of interference which conditions the stability of transmitters, the limitation of power and even of programme time. Further, broadcasting so obviously exercised its influence on public opinion that the authorities had perforce quickly to interest themselves in it. Sooner or later—and everywhere in the world—arose the question of the status that must be given broadcasting, a vital problem which may be summarized in the alternative : independence or control of the service. Different nations have solved this problem in different ways, in conformity with their political and social structure. It is on this solution, on the adopted principle of organization, that depends the whole structure of broadcasting down to the least detail of the programmes, down to the attitude of the broadcasters towards the listeners.

The Principles of Organization.

Two opposite theses prevail, that of free broadcasting, championed by private broadcasters and an important proportion of listeners, and that of a state controlled broadcasting, defended by numerous governments on technical grounds, as well as on those of national safety and defence. Between these two extremes there is the compromise of a "pliable" monopoly which limits the role of the state in the right of control and in the technical operation of transmitters. Thus three principles of organization have been elaborated:

1. *Private* ownership and operation—by individual broadcasters and commercial companies, or else by educational institutions and religious associations;

2. *Official* ownership and operation—by a national institute or a government department running broadcasting as a state service;

3. Ownership and operation by a *public utility corporation* placed under government supervision but enjoying a certain autonomy in the administration and programmes.

Most nations have adopted one of these three systems, the chief exponents of which are the United States of America, Germany and Great Britain [1]. Some countries have worked out special systems which are usually a combination or a modification of these principles. Thus, reconciling the extremes, France, Australia and Canada admit the coexistence of private and official management. Sweden, Switzerland and many other countries use a system of "double management", drawing a very clear distinction between the technical service and the programme service, the first being reserved to the state, the

---

[1] See part B, the paragraphs dealing with these countries.

second being entrusted to a broadcasting society, generally of
a semi-official character. There is yet one system which escapes
the general classification : management of stations by associations of listeners as practiced for fifteen years in the Netherlands [1].

Beside the national organizations, there are international
services, wholly differing in their character and their aims.
Placed in Europe, their activity is intended for the whole
world ; one of them was until latterly the organ of the League
of Nations [2], the other is the organ of the Vatican.

The urgent need of cooperation among broadcasters has
given birth to big international organizations ; some grouping
a great number of national broadcasting services, the others
composed of institutions, associations and personalities interested in a specific aspect of radio activity : juridical, agricultural, or religious [3].

The American System — The European System.

The principle of organization determines, as we shall see
throughout this study, the formation of the broadcast services
and of all their activities. The influence of the "régime" is
such that in America and in Europe the evolution has taken
opposite directions and one may speak today of an "American
system" and a " European system" . The first, conceding to
the radio the same rights as to the press, considers it as a
great public tribune open to all currents, to all opinions. Each
citizen, each society, each institution—"even the government"
say the Americans—can set up a station, on the one condition
that there are available frequencies. Broadcasting is free, the
authorities are content to watch over the general management

---

[1] Not being able to give a more detailed analysis of the questions
of organization, we refer the reader to our study "La Structure de
la Radiodiffusion", in the *Journal des Télécommunications*, Berne
(April, June, July, August and September 1940).

[2] Although regular broadcasts are suspended since the beginning
of the war, (*cf.* p. 137) and although this station has since been
completely taken over by a Swiss company, "Radio-Nations"
as a broadcasting organization cannot be overlooked in this
analysis.

[3] See part B IV.

and regulate the technical conditions of the service. It is the broadcasters themselves who, in order to avoid all friction with public authorities, exercise careful control over the programmes. The European system on the other hand is based on the state monopoly, on the right and the necessity of a severe control. Consequently the few existing private societies have ever been the object of constant supervision ; and no sooner had broadcasting acquired a certain importance than it was called upon to serve established authority. Generally, the government builds stations and takes on their whole management. During the last few years, and specially since the beginning of the war, official influence has been further strengthened, and numerous radio services have been taken over by the state.

One may ask—the question has frequently been put—which of these systems is preferable. The American pleads for freedom of action and freedom of speech, for the benefits of competition between rival bodies, and the pleasing of the public which receives, free of charge, what it wants. The European broadcasters thinks freedom full of dangers for national security, believes that a controlled and disinterested service can better fulfil the tasks of a public service and finally that the listener must contribute to the development of broadcasting through the payment of a tax.

Each system has advantages and disadvantages, and each one answers the interests and the political and economic conditions of the two continents. If one wished to apply the American system in Europe, it would soon be obvious that there are no financial powers great enough to put a similar service into operation ; on the other hand, the European system does not seem in harmony with American mentality, with the industrial and commercial forces of the United States which must have a free field of action in order to yield the fullest results.

Methods of Financing.

How do the hundreds of broadcasting organizations and the thousands of stations exist ? Where are obtained the millions to cover the cost of running them, what are the ever-flowing sources which allow the maintenance of so gigantic a service ? This is an extremely complicated problem, especially because of ever increasing needs. The question did not arise at first ; the pioneers of broadcasting could through their own resources set up the first stations and send out the first programmes. And enthusiastic listeners contributed voluntarily to the cost.

But that happy primitive service soon became outlived. To satisfy a public which grew more and more exacting, it was necessary to perfect and enlarge the stations, build numerous transmitters, equip studios, create radio orchestras and other artistic groups and above all ceaselessly increase the number of programmes and the broadcasting time. This evolution necessarily led to ever increasing expenses which soon outgrew the financial possibilities of the first broadcasters and of the small groups. Many of them were obliged to give up their place to commercial companies with big financial resources, to official and semi-official services aided by the state.

In order to collect the necessary funds, the American broadcasters "discovered" the sale of time for commercial advertising, introduced as early as 1923, whereas the majority of the European governments imposed upon the owners of radio receivers a "right to listen" in the form of a set tax or "licence fee". In the one system it is the advertiser who finances the service by paying for the time during which he uses the station to broadcast "his" programme ; in the other it is the listener who provides the required subsidies.

The financial system always reflects in a large measure the system of organization : it is either independent of the state depending then wholly on the success of the programmes, or it is dependent on the will of the government and more or less independent of the reactions of the public.

The main revenue of private stations—throughout the world—is derived from advertising, from the "sale of time" by the hour, the quarter of an hour and even by the minute. The receipts must not only cover the expenses of the commercial programmes themselves, but also of the sustaining programmes, broadcast during the rest of the day.

The semi-official or official service, without always scorning other contributions, relies especially on licence fees. These differ from country to country in their amount, in their form and in their application [1]. Some twenty countries collect a unique tax for all types of receivers, whatever its usage. But the majority levy taxes graduated according to the value of the sets (crystal detectors or valve receivers) ; according to the use made of them (private, public or collective) ; according to the subscribers (rural or urban, radio dealers, hotel keepers, etc.), or even according to the distance between the receiver and a central station. In the case of the private and ordinary use of a valve receiver, the annual licence fee varies between eight and thirty Swiss francs ; that for receivers in public places, from fifteen to eighty-five Swiss francs. Even subscribers to wire broadcasting services are yet obliged to pay the set tax in addition to the rather high subscriptions. Often the radio industry and trade must pay heavy taxes and duties, levied sometimes on the manufacture of receivers or accessories (particularly valves), sometimes on the sale, import, or export of radio-electrical material. When the state authorizes the operation of private stations or wire broadcasting services, these are obliged to pay licences ; the receipts either go to the treasury or are used, in part at least, by the official service. In Peru the government in addition levies 10% on every advertising contract negotiated by a private station [2]. Where licence fees are not levied or where the revenue derived from them is insufficient, the authorities grant the official services subsidies and credits, written down to the state budget.

A certain number of educational and religious stations are still today maintained by voluntary contributions of listeners ; they also enjoy the assistance of scientific and religious institutions or else of important foundations [3]. The broadcasting

---

[1] See our study "Les droits d'écoute dans le monde", *Journal des Télécommunications*, Berne, September 1939.

[2] We may note also that the services of Portugal, the Union of South Africa, British India and certain other countries count among their sources of income the fines exacted for all infringement of the legislation affecting the declaration and use of receivers, manufacture and sale of radio material, etc.

[3] The Rockefeller Foundation for instance yearly devotes very considerable sums to radio research and development, giving its support to the powerful non-commercial short-wave stations of the World Wide Broadcasting Corporation, Boston.

services of the Netherlands, run until 1940 by big associations of listeners, was solely maintained by voluntary contributions of the members.

Considerable revenue is derived from the publications of certain broadcasting societies : programme magazines which often have a very big circulation [1], annuals, hand-books, preparatory pamphlets for radio lessons sold by tens and hundreds of thousands of copies, librettos of operas and operettas, texts of broadcast talks and lectures.

Actively sharing in the artistic life of their countries, several bodies—such as the British Broadcasting Corporation, the Soviet Radio Committee, the Australian Broadcasting Commission and the official service of Uruguay—organize every season public concerts and important performances which leave to the broadcasting service a certain profit. In the U.S.A. some big companies act as "managers" of the artists and lecturers who are under permanent contract ; and the revenues of the "sale of talent" are by no means negligible.

Several broadcasting services have yet other sources of income, such as the hiring of their stations or studios, long practised by the League of Nations' service and the Dutch society PHOHI. In Iceland, by an odd exception, the government service also owns the monopoly of the sale of receivers and other radio material which it also repairs.

In many countries various sources of income are combined ; certain official services accept advertising in order to increase their income. In France there is besides the licence fee, a tax on receiving valves, in Norway a "stamp tax" (of about 10%) on the sale of radio material, in British India customs duties on the import of receivers. In Great Britain, Japan and in several British Dominions official publications and above all programme magazines yield appreciable revenue. It happens thus that the same service has two, three, four, or even five different sources of income.

Numerous countries grant considerable reductions of taxes or even total exemption to hospitals, schools, and other educational institutions. The blind, more particularly those

---

[1] The *Radio Times*, the official organ of the BBC, has a sale of three million copies a week.

without means, enjoy almost everywhere special privileges (more than 50,000 have free licences in Great Britain). The same is true of war invalids, incurables, unemployed and other destitute persons. Other reasons obtain in some countries : several concede free licences to members of the diplomatic corps and sometimes to officials ; in Greece and in Italy this privilege is granted to barracks and military centres ; in Spain to penitentiaries, to cultural and welfare institutions. The Soviet Union has freed from taxation press agencies and newspapers and—as an encouragement—radio amateurs engaged in serious experimental work. Germany, where the number of free licences already exceeds 1,200,000, exonerates the groups of the "Hitler-Jugend", the citizens who "can prove that they have rendered special service to German interest or the National-Socialist party", large families with a limited income, and receivers used in the public interest.

The private broadcaster, though having to pay taxes and commissions, can dispose of his revenues. It would be logical that this should be the case also for the official and semi-official services, especially since the licence fee is a contribution of the listeners for broadcasting. But usually they only receive part of it : in the form of taxes or other contributions, the state deducts considerable sums for the treasury or for certain government departments. Nine to twelve per cent at least go to the postal administration for expenses incurred in the collection of licences [1] or the use of telephone lines. If the post office in addition is also responsible, as is often the case, for the technical services, it keeps back a high percentage (from 40 to 60%) for the expenses of building and operating of stations ; then only the balance goes to the broadcasting company in charge of artistic and intellectual work.

Income and Expenditure.

Advertising and licence fees provide the radio with big financial means. In the United States the total of the "gross

---

[1] Only two services, in Norway and in Japan, themselves collect the licence fees.

time sales" rose between 1938-1941 from $150,118,400 to
$237,600,000 [1]. Some twenty advertisers each paid in 1940
more than one million dollars to the chief broadcasting companies (NBC and CBS) ; two of them devoted more than four
millions to radio advertising, two others nearly six millions,
and one firm even $10,999,416 [2]. The sale of time is also an
excellent proposition for the private Australian stations, the
commercial service of New-Zealand—run for several years now
by the state—and also for the official Canadian broadcasting
society. The licence fees produced, in 1939 [3], 470,682,360 francs
in France [4], £4,500,000 in Great Britain and about 300 million
marks in Germany. Even in smaller and less populated countries
the tax yields considerable revenue : in Switzerland for instance, 8,147,000 Swiss francs in 1939 and 10 millions in 1941.

The voluntary contributions and subscriptions of the Dutch
listeners were also extremely high and for one association
(the AVRO) amounted to more than 710,000 florins ; further,
850,000 florins were derived from the sale of the programme
magazine, and a major part of this sum was used for the expenses
of the service [5]. The net revenues from the sale of publications
increased the income of the BBC, by £846,094 in 1937 and 1938 ;
and the entrance tickets for the performances organized by
the Australian Broadcasting Commission yielded £55,214 in
the last pre-war financial year.

These are indeed enormous figures, but necessary to cover
the multifarious running expenses : administration and staff
salaries ; the operation of stations and studios ; technical
improvements and the extension of networks ; the use of the
telephone lines connecting the studio to the stations and
linking these together ; the programmes service and all that

---

[1] See *Broadcasting Yearbooks*, 1939-42.

[2] According to an analysis of the NBC Research Division. See
Broadcasting, July 21, 1941, p. 54.

[3] This is the last year in which the revenues of the three great
European nations can be compared.

[4] Information of Paul Allard in *Le Matin*, Paris, quoted by the
Rundfunkarchiv, Berlin, April 1941, p. 148.

[5] The Dutch associations were thus able to cover their expenses,
and it is only for political reasons that in 1941 the voluntary
contributions were replaced by licence fees.

it implies ; taxes and commissions ; finally innumerable minor items, from correspondence with the listener to the regular contributions which must be paid to international broadcasting organizations.

First we may quote some figures from the U.S.A. : the networks and 765 stations—having in 1940 a total revenue of $147,146,717 [1]—had to spend $113,850,009 for their services ; half the sum went to appointments and salaries. According to FCC statistics, the staff, numbering 21,646 persons, received in one week $1,019,548, that is an average of $47.13, an average higher than that of any other American industry.

The British Broadcasting Corporation devoted £3,534,795 to its service in 1938; the programmes took £1,892,081 (of which £218,310 for the BBC's permanent orchestras) and £673,855 for the technical service. £208,196 had further to be paid in taxes. The budget for 1940/41 was fixed at £4,500,000 of which £620,000 were reserved entirely for broadcast in foreign languages [2]. In the financial year 1939/40 the Swiss broadcasting society spent 4,518,901 francs on programmes, studios, and administration, to which must be added 3,747,000 francs for the technical service, for the payment of interest and amortization of installations.

If the major part of the revenues is devoted to programmes, at least in the well organized services, high sums are often absorbed by secondary expenses. Thus in 1938 the BBC had to earmark £389,274 for performing rights and copyright, representing 10.24% of its total revenue ; and the Canadian Broadcasting Corporation 20% of the total expenditure on wire line charges for carrying programmes on the national system ; the collection of taxes, a very burdensome task, cost the Japanese society (in the same period) 2,653,463 Yen, thus more than two-thirds of the sum devoted to programmes.

In spite of all expenditures, certain services show considerable profits and succeed in creating important reserve funds which allow them to meet the unforeseen. In 1940 the excess of income over expenditures of the American networks and stations was $33,296,708 ; the Australian

---

[1] After deduction of commissions amounting to $ 20,859,018.

[2] In February 1942 a special credit of £ 1,300,000 was granted to the BBC to extend its Overseas Services.

Broadcasting Commission was able to transfer £47,254 into its reserve funds which amounted then to £476,895.

But the expenses of broadcasting increase year by year. The extension of networks, the building of powerful stations and of big studios demand vast capital, and television, even before becoming generalized, has already cost millions of dollars.

II. TRANSMISSION

Once the problem of organization had been solved in one way or another, the technical problem arose. Broadcasting, the disorganized beginnings of which nearly led to chaos, had to be regulated and given laws. It became necessary to provide political and cultural centres with transmitters and to "cover" the entire area of each country. Obstacles of all kinds—reasons of topography and climate, social and economic conditions, political and regional tendencies, particularly the use of several languages in one country—hindered, and often enough hinder today, the fulfilment of this task. The most serious obstacle however is a strictly technical one : the limited number of available air channels.

Distribution of Wave Lengths.

When radio broadcasting came into being, the ether was already overcrowded. The frequencies which it needed were long since in use by the services working for national defence, rescue at sea, commercial transactions and rapid communications. The place conceded to broadcasting, seven years after its birth, at the International Radiotelegraph Conference in Washington in 1927 soon became too small and is so still, in spite of later concessions made by other radio communication services and in spite of the often very ingenious technical solutions. For in all and for every purpose broadcasting has at its disposal only several frequency bands with a total of 3465 kilocycles divided into three groups[1] :

long waves : 160 to 265 kc/s or 1875 to 1132 metres
medium waves : 550 to 1560 kc/s or 545.5 to 192.3 metres
(standard broadcast band)
short waves : eight bands with 2350 frequencies between 6000 and 26.600 kc/s or 50 and 11.28 metres.

---

[1] Figures of the International Telecommunication Union.

— 28 —

The last of these bands however, from 25.600 to 26.600 kc/s
(or from 11.72 to 11.28 metres) is not very favourable and up
to the present hardly used ; consequently, about one thousand frequencies are lost.

Owing to climatic conditions three bands of *intermediate
waves* have been allotted to broadcasting in the tropical zone[1]:

2300 to 2500 kc/s	130.4 to 120 m
3300 to 3500 kc/s	90.91 to 85.71 m
4770 to 4965 kc/s	62.89 to 60.42 m

Granted that a minimum separation of 9 to 10 kc/s is
necessary between the stations to avoid interference, it is
extremely difficult to place all the stations—a few transmitters
apart [2]—over these few bands. In order to solve this problem
and ensure the national and international broadcasting service
it has been necessary to establish regional plans for the
allocation of wave lengths and make various arrangements :
the formation of networks, of which all the affiliated stations,
or at least a part of them, broadcast the same programme on the
same channel ; the sharing of wave lengths by distant stations;
the sharing of broadcasting time by the transmitters in the
same region : and finally the limitation of power for the
majority of stations.

It is not our task to set out the technical laws of broadcasting
nor to examine the numerous national, regional, and international agreements and regulations ; many engineering and
legal experts have written enlightened studies on these
questions [3]. For readers less familiar with these problems it
should be said that each group of wave lengths has special

---

[1] Between latitude 30° north and latitude 30° south.

[2] Benefiting from concessions of other radio-electrical services.

[3] We would like to cite among others : John H. Morecroft
Principles of Radio Communication, New York 1937 ; W.T.
O'Dea *Radio Communication*, Publications of the Science Museum,
London 1934 ; W.L. Everitt *Communication Engineering*, New
York 1937. — C.B. Joliffe "Practical Limitation of the Broadcast
Allocation Structure" in *Educational Broadcasting* 1936, pp. 64-76
H. Giess "Die Entwicklung der Weltnachrichtenverträge"
in *Studien zum Weltrundfunk und Fernsehrundfunk*, vol. II,
Heidelberg 1941 ; J.D. Tomlinson *The International Control of
Radiocommunications*, Geneva 1938 ; J. Stewart "The Madrid
International Telecommunication Convention" in *Air Law
Review*, July 1934, p. 236-266.

qualities and characteristics, especially where propagation through the air is concerned ; short waves for instance are particularly suited to long distance transmission and are thus appropriate to the broadcasting of international programmes. It should further be added that the allocation of wave lengths appertains on the one hand to the International Telecommunication Conferences, which distribute the frequency bands to the various radiocommunication services, and on the other hand to regional conferences which attribute frequencies available for broadcasting to countries of a certain zone. Thanks to the allocation plans and the technical measures consequent upon these, it has been possible to maintain order in the domain of long and medium wave lengths. For short waves however there is no such plan and it would besides be very difficult to establish considering the special character of these waves—which require a world plan—and the rapidly growing needs of national services.

From time to time plans are modified and adapted to technical progress and to the development of services. At the present time broadcasting is organized by the General Radiocommunication Regulations [1] (revision of Cairo 1938) annexed to the International Telecommunication Convention (Madrid 1932) ; the European Broadcasting Convention, Lucerne 1933 [1] and the plan annexed to the Convention [2] ; the North American Regional Broadcasting Agreement [3], signed at Havana in 1937 but in force only since March 29, 1941 [4] ; finally by several regional agreements between the states of South America and between those of Central America [5]. These conventions are observed even in war-time—apart from the "jamming" of propaganda broadcasts and certain temporary

[1] Text published by the Bureau of the International Telecommunication Union.

[2] The "Plan of Lucerne" was to be replaced by the "Plan of Montreux" adopted in 1939 ; but its application foreseen for March 4, 1940 has been postponed owing to the political situation.

[3] Cf. Broadcasting Yearbook, 1941, pp. 398-407.

[4] Owing to the belated ratification of Mexico. The application of the "Havana Treaty" obliged about 1,300 North American stations to change their wave lengths.

[5] See Journal des Télécommunications, Berne 1935, pp. 110, 125 ; 1937, pp. 287-294 ; 1940, pp. 89-101 and 198-199; 1941 pp. 82-86.

alterations of wave lengths due above all to military reasons—since these plans of allocation serve not only the interests of services, but are also conditioned by the technical laws and necessities.

Although any decision in this field is largely determined by considerations of a technical nature, the principle of organization greatly influences the distribution of broadcasting stations. Commercial companies whose aim is to reach large audiences with their advertising programmes prefer to have their stations in big towns, in the most thickly populated and rich districts ; public authorities on the contrary, anxious to give all people the possibility of benefiting by broadcasting, endeavour to reach the remotest corners of the country. Consequently the private networks only touch towns or regions whose population has a big purchasing power whereas the official networks place if possible a central station and several relay stations in each province. Thus we find in certain countries with private systems, vast territories entirely deprived of transmitters beside towns overcrowded with rival stations—Mexico City and Montevideo have as many as 30 and Havana 41.

Often the number of stations and their power does not correspond either to the needs of a country or to the number of listeners : in the Dominican Republic for instance there are hardly 7,000 receivers and no less than 18 transmitters ; very powerful stations operate in the small frontier towns of Mexico with the United States as their aim. In order to rectify the inconveniences of a distribution of stations derived entirely from commercial interests, several Latin American governments have in the last few years built important official stations.

Geographical and climatic conditions, technical development and progress, national and commercial reasons and furthermore the wishes of a public anxious to choose between several programmes of a different nature—all these factors have led to the building of stations and the gradual increase of their power.

2,836 Transmitters.

A serried network is spread today over the earth. Night and day hundreds, thousands of stations broadcast words and music through the world. In 1920 a start was made in America

with two stations, in 1922 with 7 in Europe. In 1926 there were
995 and nearly 2,000 ten years later. At the beginning of 1942
there were 2,832 transmitters in the world [1]. They are distributed as follows :

Continents	Long and medium waves	Intermediate and short waves	Total
North and Central America	1280	118	1398
South America	362	146	508
Europe (including U.S.S.R. and Turkey)	406	66	472
Asia [2]	132	84	216
Oceania	156	9	165
Africa	46	31	77
	2382	454	2836

The United States of America who alone have 902 stations
occupy the first place, they are followed by Mexico with 153
stations (166 transmitters), by Australia with 129 stations,
Cuba with 102, Canada with 95, Brazil with 86, the Soviet
Union with 79, Colombia and Venezuela with 75 transmitters
each. Germany which in the former territory of the Reich
only possessed 30 stations, exploits or controls nearly 100
stations in the annexed, occupied or incorporated territories.
Similarly Japan which has 47 transmitters controls thirteen
transmitters in (Chosen) Corea and (Taiwan) Formosa, some
twenty of the Chinese stations, numerous stations in the
Dutch East Indies, in Hongkong, Thailand, Malaya, and indi-
rectly at least, the 22 transmitters of Mandchukuo.

The number of stations however is not the only essential
factor in gauging the importance and the capacity of a broadcasting service. Equally significant is their power. It is thence

---

[1] Figures based on documents of the International Telecommunication Union, the International Broadcasting Union, the
Federal Communications Commission, Washington, the U.S.
Department of Commerce and the *Broadcasting Yearbook*, 1941.
It is hardly possible to give with absolute precision the number
of stations in use, the fluctuations being at the present time very
great and the data of certain countries incomplete. Moreover
there are many stations which, owing to political events, have
been shut down or destroyed, whereas others created for military
reasons have not been officially mentioned.

[2] Not including about 60 small private stations in China ; these
scarcely operate today.

that derives that "race for power" which began ten years ago and which is by no means finished today. Whereas in 1926 a station of 3 kilowatts was considered as very "powerful", in 1930 a station of 50 kW was in no way exceptional. The total aerial power had been more than tripled during that period rising from 1,055 to 3,247 kW ; for Europe alone statistics show an increase from 268.5 to 1,813.9 kW [1]. Today there are no less than 185 high-powered stations [2] : of those there is one of 500 kW, Moscow Komintern, one of 450 kW, Radio-Paris [3], one of 200 kW, Radio-Luxemburg, nine of 150 kW, twelve of 120-125 kW, forty of 100 kW, twenty-four of 60 to 80 kW and over eighty of 50 kW.

Among these stations twenty-two work on short waves and for foreign and distant countries. This fact and the large number of transmitters using frequencies above 6000 kc—nearly 340— clearly show the importance of short-wave radio and consequently of international broadcasting. Some of these big stations are genuine "transmission centres" each formed of a group of powerful transmitters : for instance the Daventry Empire Station has eight transmitters of 50 to 100 kW provided with 25 directional antennae and using some 40 frequencies ; its rival station, the "Deutscher Kurzwellensender" at Zeesen which was greatly enlarged for the broadcasting of the Olympic Games in 1936, also has some ten transmitters using, with 12 to 50 kW, from 25 to 30 frequencies ; the Moscow short-wave centre (RW 96) broadcasts with 100 kW on 24 frequencies and with 15 kW on 22 other frequencies. There are also very important short-wave stations at Rome-Prato Smeraldo and the Vatican City, at Geneva-Prangins and Schwarzen- burg (Switzerland), at Allouis (France), Kootwijk and Huizen (Netherlands), Podiebrad (Bohemia and Moravia), at Tokyo, Chungking, New-Delhi and Sydney. The eleven "international stations" of the United States rank among the most powerful

---

[1] Figures based on the statistics of the IBU.

[2] The number is probably even higher owing to the strengthening of certain stations and the building of new ones in the belligerent countries. Their opening and the power used are not announced for military reasons.

[3] Power given in the Montreux Plan.

in the world, those of Bound Brook WRCA and of Schenectady WGEO having 100 kW, that of Mason, Ohio 75 kW, and the others mostly 50 kW.

The application of short and intermediate waves has also allowed the solution of certain problems which before seemed insoluble, such as that of broadcasting in the tropics where the long and medium waves are so seriously affected by atmospherics that during the greater part of the year the reception of them is practically impossible. Thanks to the short waves, broadcasting in Latin America, so long delayed, could at last be developed. There are there today more than 245 stations working on short and intermediate waves ; in some countries such as Ecuador, Peru, Venezuela and the Dominican Republic they outnumber the stations working on the standard broadcast band, in other countries such as Honduras and Nicaragua, all stations use short waves. The number and the power of short-wave stations constantly increases and hardly a month passes without the opening of a new one [1]. And with the adoption of ultra-high frequencies, with television and frequency modulation broadcasting [2], the broadcaster faces new horizons.

The transmitting station is complemented by the receiving station, thus making it possible to enrich the programmes with material broadcast by other home or foreign stations. To these should now be added the monitoring stations responsible for the control of foreign broadcasts, in particular news bulletins. Their activity is of the utmost importance not only for governments and their propaganda departments, but also for broadcasting services which are thus in a position to gather a great deal of information.

National and International Networks.

The desire to increase the reach and the scope of programmes and to serve wider regions, has led private and official broadcasters to form regional and national networks. By linking

---

[1] This progress is however a source of great concern for technicians, certain bands such as that of 49 m being already crowded and interference being thus inevitable.

[2] See Part C.

the stations one to another by telephone circuits [1] it became possible to broadcast at the same hour the same programme throughout the country and thus increase not only the number of listeners but also the value of advertising and the effect of a government broadcast.

Here again the example was set by America where three stations in New York City, Providence R.I. and Cincinnati formed themselves in 1924 into a group which, greatly enlarged, became two years later the foundation of the first network : the National Broadcasting Company (NBC). Four huge chains cross today the territory of the United States, the Red Network of the NBC with a total of 130 stations, the Blue Network with 116 stations [2], the network of the Columbia Broadcasting System (CBS) with 127 stations, and that of the Mutual Broadcasting System (MBS) whose power is less but which has nearly 200 stations. In the European countries too, particularly in Great Britain, Germany, France, Italy, Finland and Sweden, the national stations were made into networks. So too the official stations in Japan, New Zealand, Australia and Canada form long chains, the two latter closely cooperating with the private stations. Finally groups of commercial stations in the Argentine, Brazil, Cuba and Mexico have formed networks in order to pool the broadcasting of advertising programmes.

Experience has shown that, the remarkable developments of long distance transmissions notwithstanding, the surest way of reaching listeners is still through the broadcasting of a programme by the favourite local station. Consequently several companies in the United States have, with the co-operation of Latin American broadcasters, established in 1941 vast "systems" of stations relaying their programmes, most often transmitted by short-waves. Thus to the national networks are today added several international networks which are intended to promote—by means of the organized broadcasting of programmes throughout the two Americas—the feeling of a Pan-American community [3]. The biggest of them,

---

[1] They are today in the United States, Canada, Australia and even in Sweden and in Switzerland tens of thousands of kilometres long.

[2] Until 1941 the Blue Network was also run by the NBC but it is now run as an autonomous company.

[3] See also Part A III, Programmes.

the *NBC Pan-American Network*, comprises in Latin America 124 short and medium wave stations which have agreed to rebroadcast the programmes of the company's big international stations WRCA and WNBI at Bound Brook ; the *CBS Latin American Network* has 76 stations representing each of the 20 republics and carrying the programmes of the short wave stations WCBX and WCRC at Brentwood, Long Island ; finally the *Cadena Radio Inter-Americana*, founded by the Crosley Corporation, has 28 stations which transmit programmes originating from Cincinnati and broadcast by WLWO in Mason, Ohio. A similar system has long since been organized in the British Empire where many stations relayed every week—daily since the beginning of the war—the programmes of the BBC Overseas Transmitters at Daventry.

Studios and Broadcasting Centres.

Technical needs, the necessity of building stations and networks, caused the arranging of studios and other such premises to be neglected for a long time. But the constant development of programmes, in quantity as well as in quality, demanded that makeshift premises be replaced by modern studios, adapted to special requirements and, in their size and acoustics, appropriate to the different kinds of broadcasts. The increasing number of collaborators, the regular participation of a large number of performers, required more space. In order that a more living atmosphere be created through the presence of a "public", accommodation had to be made for hundreds of spectator-listeners [1]. Today every important society owns a set of studios of varying sizes—from the speaker's small cabin to the vast concert hall intended for big orchestras and choirs—and linked sometimes to five, six or even eleven studios for a single radio-theatrical programme.

The development of broadcasting, the extension and variety of its activities have since 1931 led to the creation of "headquarters" grouping all the necessary services. In most of the

---

[1] The main studios in Berlin and New York have even from 1,100 to 1,500 seats.

world's capitals there is today a broadcasting house, symbolic of the power of the radio. Thousands of programmes are broadcast from these centres, from the sky-scraper of the "Radio-City" in New York housing, together with the other branches of the Radio Corporation of America, the entire services of the NBC and the Blue Network Company ; from the magnificent "Broadcasting House" in London [1] ; from the impressive "Haus des Rundfunks" in Berlin ; from the luxurious buildings in Vienna and in Rome; from the Brussels centre, conceived as a true "factory of sound " ; from the new auditoria in five Swiss towns, and the immense buildings of the Japanese radio at Tokyo and Osaka.

Auxiliary Equipment.

Various auxiliary equipment is required for the programme service, especially for running commentaries, radio-theatre and music. It ranges from motorcars or even specially equipped aeroplanes to the film and instruments for sound-effects. Most important of these is the recording apparatus which permits to preserve on records (of wax or glass) or on a film (sound film or steel ribbon) a topical event, a speech, a noteworthy artistic performance, or else the sounds and noises of the "sound background" of radio plays. It is thus possible to postpone the transmission of programmes to the most appropriate time and that is specially valuable for the international broadcasting which is obliged to take into account the difference of time zones between the continents. For many years every important broadcast has been kept in the special archives of the big radio societies [2]. The BBC also records numerous programmes in order to send them to some of the Dominions and Colonies which cannot always receive the broadcasts direct from the Daventry Empire Station.

---

[1] Although heavily bombarded several times the building as a whole has remained intact and continues to serve the British radio.

[2] Thus an important station of the Mutual Broadcasting System (Newark WOR) possesses a big collection of recordings referring to the history and the "prehistory" of the present war. It includes all the broadcast speeches of famous statesmen and in addition all the international news bulletins. *cf. Bulletin IBU,* August 1941, p. 256.

At all times the broadcasting service must have at its disposal technical publications, rich musical and literary material and an extensive choice of gramophone records. Broadcasting centres therefore have special collections : libraries containing thousands of books and periodicals dealing with radio, stage and radio plays and specially big collections of records containing, as is the case for instance with the German radio, about 140,000 items (80,000 records and 60,000 electrical transcriptions). The musical collection of the British radio, one of the richest in the world, comprises—60,000 records apart—all the scores necessary for 23,000 orchestral works (of which 7,000 are in duplicate and 2,000 in triplicate) ; 100,000 vocal scores ; 20,000 songs ; 4,000 pieces of military music ; 1,500 for chamber music; 60,000 for various solo instruments (piano, organ, violin, etc.) and finally 8,000 manuscripts.

Wire Broadcasting.

Beside direct broadcasting, certain countries apply an intermediary method : *wire broadcasting*[1], that is distribution by wire of programmes by means of "relay exchanges" (central receiving stations) using telephone lines or circuits specially adapted.

The advantages—and indeed the justification—of this method of transmission are the elimination, to a considerable extent at least, of disturbances, the suppression of fading and the maintenance of a uniform sound level. There is another advantage in a certain saving of expense for the listener who thus no longer needs a receiving set but only the loud-speaker. This explains the favourable development of wire broadcasting in spite of such inconveniences as the limited choice of programmes (five at the maximum) and the often very high rates of subscription. This method has been adopted particularly in mountain regions and in certain towns where direct reception is seriously hindered, as in Switzerland, in the big towns of the Netherlands, and in the capital of Hungary.

---

[1] Known also under the technical term "telediffusion".

Innumerable relay exchanges also operate in the Soviet Union where wire transmission has been introduced by the government since a major part of the population is not able to buy a receiver and because, for political and cultural reasons, the government favours collective listening.

III. Programmes

As the technical and financial means developed, so also did the possibilities, the aims and the tasks of broadcasting. The public, the ordinary listener, is hardly aware of these tasks —they are multifarious and greatly surpass those of any other organization. Never in the history of human culture has there existed an institution popularizing every day, for ten, fifteen and sometimes twenty-four hours intellectual and artistic matter, working for the benefit of an audience so vast and so different in traditions, opinions, taste and level of culture.

Much has been written on the difficulties which arise from the fact that the radio public is "blind" and on the necessity of removing from the microphone everything that is not audible. We may therefore limit ourselves to the mere mention of these difficulties as well as of those which arise from the racial, denominational and social divergences of the public, from its national and regional sentiments and particularly from the diversity of languages. These differences in the audience—further divided according to the preference for the serious or the light—condition the variety of broadcasts and lead to an ever greater extension of the programme service.

In the first days of broadcasting listeners were delighted by programmes which would be described today as "ridiculous". But the more they were given, the more they asked. To meet the requirements of the public it soon became necessary to broadcast "alternative" programmes : comedy at the same time as tragedy, operettas at the same time as symphony concerts. Stations had to be equipped with two transmitters capable of broadcasting different programme material ; further, it became necessary to form double networks, such as the NBC Red and Blue Networks or the "national" and "regional" networks of the BBC. The Italian stations were grouped into several chains, carrying programmes from different transmission centres ; France applied for the evening programmes a plan by which five types of broadcasts alternated between five groups of official stations (serious music ; light and operatic music ; drama ; variety ; relays) [1].

Moreover, special programmes intended for certain sections of the population had to be arranged ; for listeners of different ages (children, adolescents, adults), for women and for men, for peasants, workers or soldiers, for the faithful of different religions and also for the sick and the blind. Taking differences of language into account, Switzerland and Belgium have assigned one of the main languages to each of their main stations. Finally, national programmes apart, broadcasts had to be devised for listeners living in the colonies or abroad.

These needs complicated but also enriched the setting-up of programmes which today touch all the domains of life. One of the most important results was the constant increase of broadcasting time and of the number of programmes : before the war, 70 Soviet stations speaking 65 languages and dialects, worked about 120,000 hours a year ; in 1939 the 17 British stations about the same numbers of hours—43,198 hours being reserved for over-sea programmes [2]—whereas the 28 national stations of Australia even totalled 149,855 hours [3]. The record however is held by the stations of the United States, where the majority work 15 hours a day and even more.

Contrarily perhaps to one's expectations, the war has not reduced the service. For, whereas home programmes in the belligerent countries have been simplified and reduced and the broadcasting day now ends in many European countries at 9 or 10 p.m., special programmes have been greatly developed. The services of the belligerent and the neutral countries have introduced "Programmes for the Forces" and multiplied, for reasons of political and economic propaganda, the so-called "international" broadcasts. During the first year of the war,

---

[1] See *La Radiodiffusion, Puissance Mondiale*, p. 107.
[2] *BBC Handbook*, 1940, p. 10-11.
[3] Annual Report of the ABC, 1939-40.

the German radio totalled 114,224 hours of broadcasts in German ; to these should be added the transmissions of the short-wave service, whose transmitters worked 111 ¹/₄ hours a day, offering 91 news bulletins and 38 talks in foreign languages [1].

Composition of Programmes.

The composition of programmes is determined both by the will of broadcasters and by the wishes of listeners. But there is a marked difference according to the principle of organization. The private broadcaster whose existence and success depend on the success of advertising broadcasts, conceives his programmes on lines calculated to give complete satisfaction to the majority as well as to the smallest groups served by special stations ; the official broadcaster, or the state broadcasting service, pursues a radio policy which conforms with the government's policy and seeks to lead the people in a given direction. Thus "variety" is the slogan of the private stations : entertainment, the "lighter side", predominates in their programmes. On the other hand the programmes of official stations favour information, instruction and also serious music. This does not mean however that the private broadcaster sets the serious element aside, that he shirks his responsibilities ; nor does this mean that the national service neglects the needs of the general public.

The character of a broadcasting service is, of course, closely related to the political structure of a country. Thus, in peacetime at least, independence in broadcasting is revealed in the freedom of speech ; allegiance to public authority, in the more or less "inspired" utterances which in the totalitarian states are at the service of political propaganda. In war-time the conception "liberal or authoritarian" has often given place to that of "neutral or belligerent".

Present events and the passionate interest that they excite even in countries which are far removed from the theatre of

---

[1] See *Der Schweizerische Rundspruch*, Berne, February 19, 1941.

war have been favourable to the *information service* in all its forms : news bulletins and commentaries, communiqués and messages, the spoken newspaper, reports of current events, relays of important speeches and political meetings; generally limited at the most to one fifth of the programme, information forms today, if not the principal, certainly the essential part of the programme. A comparison of statistics gives significant results. In Germany programmes of information, current events and propaganda claimed in 1935 an average of 912 hours a month or 16.5% of the total broadcasting time ; in 1940, in one month (April), the German stations broadcast news programmes during 3,068 hours, during nearly 31% of the total time. This development is even more clearly illustrated by the detailed figures for spoken broadcasts which reveal the increasing proportion of time reserved for information. It rose from 70.4% at the beginning of 1939 to 78.1% after the outbreak of the war and to 83.1% in the last quarter of 1940 ; in the same period, literary broadcasts fell from 14.7 to 6.8 and finally to 3.1%. The same development, though to a lesser degree, may be seen in a neutral country such as Sweden where information took 41.7%, 44.5% and 48.2% of the spoken broadcasts[1]. Where Australia is concerned, the time devoted to news bulletins and commentaries increased from 7,700 hours in 1938/39 to 18.206 in the following year.

For a long time the press has been fighting against the radio, trying to hinder and delay its progress. This was a useless opposition which began to subside when both groups realized that, in fact, they acted as stimulants upon each other, and that they could and must work hand in hand[2]. Nowadays, with the exception of a few countries, the radio and the press cooperate in the task of giving information.

While, before the war, broadcasting stations took but little interest in military matters—except in the authoritarian states where the military training of the young was preached—today these questions have moved into the front rank. Everywhere the radio is called upon to serve the cause of national defence

---

[1] Figures based on statistics of the IBU.

[2] Since Dec. 1, 1941 "last-minute news" gathered by the *New York Times* is broadcast every hour on the hour by WMCA, a leading New York station.

and to stimulate the interest of the nation for the army. Radio in wartime, the president of the NAB stated, has three main roles : to cooperate with the government in recruiting workers, soldiers and sailors ; to stimulate the sale of defence bonds and stamps ; and to help build up and maintain public morale.

News bulletins and political broadcasts apart, there are innumerable other kinds of information, commentaries and reports of sporting events, exchange rates and market prices, weather forecasts and time signals, indications about road conditions, warnings to ships, information and advice of all types, especially on the occasion of catastrophic events and bad weather.

The radio assists the police, pursues criminals, seeks the lost and calls for assistance in cases of illness or accident. Moreover it appeals to people's generosity for philanthropic and humanitarian work. In 1940 the appeals made by the BBC stations for the "Week's Good Cause" brought in £355,434.

Yet in our time *music* still remains the chief element in programmes, taking up at the minimum 50% of broadcasting time. Japan alone gives music 10% ; Finland, Sweden, and Hungary are somewhat below the average. In Portugal music reaches 78.5% and in certain Latin American countries even more. Light music (operettas, songs, dance music) reigns everywhere, but all big stations nevertheless foster serious music : the opera, symphonic and choral works, and more rarely chamber music. Aware of their cultural responsibilities they also follow the wishes of a by no means negligible proportion of listeners [1].

Literary programmes which are less suitable for the general public, have been introduced rather slowly, being for a long time limited to 4-6%. But thanks to their often remarkably high standard their share of time has considerably increased.

---

[1] Eloquent protests were made to the BBC and also to "Radio-Genève" when they suppressed part of the transmissions of symphony concerts ; the recent referendum organized by the Italian radio showed that 86% of the listeners voted for opera and 40%, that is 347,371 listeners, for symphony concerts. What better proof of the attraction of good music is needed than the example of an American firm of oil products which has for fourteen years offered a symphony concert every week ?

This development is due chiefly to the success of the new forms of radio theatre, varying from plays specially written for broadcasting to adaptations of stage plays, novels, short stories, biographies and films.

The place accorded to *lectures and talks* varies considerably from country to country. Starting from 5 to 6% in the Argentine and Germany, the figure rises to 13% in Denmark, to 15.87% in Sweden and reaches 23% in Japan.

Words and music are closely allied in revues and musical comedies, in feature programmes (a highly developed form), in music lessons and numerous special transmissions. Such "mixed programmes" accounted in 1940 for 1.7% of the total in Denmark, for 4.4% in Germany, for 7.3% in Sweden and for over 12% in Italy.

Recorded Programmes.

A major part of all these broadcasts is recorded. Records and electrical transcriptions are alone able to satisfy the requirements of the services, especially where musical programmes are concerned. They make possible the solution of the problems of a delayed or repeated transmission and effect considerable economy. The percentage of such recordings is very high and in many countries it reaches a fifth or a third of the programmes. In the year 1939/40 the national service of Australia broadcast 411,793 recorded items, that is 61.6% of the total. Certain stations in Latin America use gramophone records almost exlusively owing to their limited financial means or the lack of local talent. On the other hand the best organized services prefer "living" performances : the Danish radio had thus limited (in 1937/38) the broadcasting of records to 2,6% or 130 hours for the whole year. Many stations are not content with the recordings of the gramophone industry, but themselves record many musical and spoken broadcasts. Thus in Germany (in the last quarter of 1939) 38.1% of the recorded programmes, that is 1500 hours, were done by the radio service itself, and in Italy all such programmes.

Radio Advertising.

This analysis of programmes would be incomplete without the mention of certain special activities.

Among these the first place is held by radio advertising, practised on a very large scale in America and Oceania but excluded, or at least greatly limited, in the majority of the European countries.

There are two different forms :   direct publicity which consists mainly of a detailed announcement, and indirect publicity which uses attractive programmes to capture the attention of the listener on behalf of a some briefly mentioned product.   The first form prevails in the local stations, particularly in Latin America where numerous advertisements are inserted between the records ;   the second is specially used by the powerful stations and the big networks in the United States.

The commercial programme has many different forms, from a recorded song to a symphony concert, or the relay of an opera, from a small sketch to a sensational report of a sporting event.   Since the war some advertisers prefer to offer news bulletins and political commentaries, being thus sure to reach an attentive public.

Wherever advertising is adopted without restrictions, its part in the programme is considerable :   in the United States commercial programmes account for about a third of the broadcasting time ;   in Latin America the spoken advertisements sometimes take up 20% of programme time.

There is no need to discuss here the pros and cons of radio advertising.   Its excesses cannot but be deprecated, though its importance and influence cannot be denied ; it is a valuable help to the radio services and acts as a stimulant in the economic life.

Education by Radio.

At the opposite pole of the commercial programme is the educational programme, promoted both by official stations and many private ones.   Though still used insufficiently, educational broadcasting already exercises a great influence.

Its elementary form is that of school broadcasting. Assisting the teacher in his task it gives—as a subsidiary means of teaching—impressions and knowledge that the school cannot give the pupils.   The choice of themes and the manner of their presentation is boundless ; according to a British expert the most suitable programmes are those which sound least like lessons. Experience has shown also that nothing is more effective than the dramatization of a subject, whenever that is possible.

One after the other the radio services have, with the support of educational authorities, introduced school broadcasts. Their number increases in significant proportions as does the number of pupils who benefit from them. In the first term of 1940 the BBC, which has always shown active interest in this work, devoted to schools 780 programmes lasting on an average twenty minutes and divided into thirty categories ; the German radio (in 1939) offered 2,583 broadcasts for schools, averaging 28 minutes each, and the Australian Broadcasting Commission 3,000 programmes of fifteen minutes [1]. As the broadcasts increased, hundreds and thousands of schools were provided with receivers : more than 10,000 in Great Britain, Germany and Belgium, over 20,000 in Italy with a total of 3,362,254 pupils. In Japan 17,000 schools with 7,310,000 pupils have receiving installations [2].

But nowhere is school broadcasting more developed than in the United States where hundreds of stations broadcast special programmes for the schools ; in 1938 already 80,000 schools with 7,000,000 pupils followed more or less regularly the programmes offered by the national networks. The most characteristic example of this activity is the "American School of the Air" founded in 1930 by the Columbia Broadcasting System. Constantly enlarged and enjoying a prodigious success, it serves as a model for the Schools of the Air recently set up in several Latin American countries.

In order to increase the effectiveness of the broadcasts and add weight to the teaching, the written word accompanies the spoken. Many broadcasting organizations publish, their commented programmes apart, small pamphlets intended to prepare for and supplement the broadcast ; these are distributed free to schools or sold at a very small price.

---

[1] cf. "School Broadcasting in 1939", annex to the *Bulletin IBU*, August 1940.
[2] *Ibidem.*

The Children's Hour which is related to the school radio also serves educational ends, though in a more entertaining form. It has real importance when, as in England, it endeavours to interest children in the innumerable facts that they can and must understand, or when, as in Japan, it enters into the daily life of the children. In war-time, these programmes also sometimes serve as a means of contact between parents and evacuated children.

But educational work is not limited to children, it also aims at the intellectual and artistic development of adults. The influence of school broadcasting is continued in the post-school teaching, in the broadcasts intended for young students. In the United States and in some European countries university courses by eminent teachers are broadcast for them.

The programmes include a wealth of instructive lecturing, courses on foreign languages, talks on all aspects of life, science and the arts, capable of interesting listeners. The Women's Hour particularly, offering much useful information, has become usual in every programme. The four major networks of the United States reserve an important proportion of their broadcasts to educational programmes. Some forty universities and colleges, which own stations, share their teaching with thousands of listeners ; finally numerous educational institutions and associations take an active interest in broadcasting. For the last ten years the official stations of Mexico and the Uruguay have pursued a fruitful educational activity, intended not only for school-children, but also for teachers, for parents and for the general public.

The proof that this educational work meets the real needs of listeners has been given time and again by their correspondence with broadcasting services, by the registrations for language lessons, by the requests for preparatory pamphlets, by the work sent to the director of radio courses for correction and revision, and lastly by the results of the inquiries which reveal how many listeners wish to be taught by the radio. A few examples, taken among hundreds, must suffice : the NBC annually dis-, tributes a million booklets to American schools, the BBC sold 2,500,000 copies in 1939. On the occasion of a recent inquiry in Italy[1] 371,210 listeners asked for educational broadcasts

---

[1] "Referendum EIAR" 1940.

on various subjects ; nearly 50,000 wanted lessons in foreign languages, 24,696 elementary courses in agriculture, while 21,295 were interested in radio technique and 12,292 in mechanics.

This clearly revealed interest has prompted the services to organize special broadcasts for groups of listeners ready to follow them regularly, discuss the subjects, and actively participate in the programmes [1].

A particularly fruitful activity is that of broadcasts for professions. Tried succesfully in Czechoslovakia, Poland and the Soviet Union they were adopted by many European services who keep daily one or several hours for programmes intended for instance for workmen, tradesmen, craftsmen, and dealing with questions which especially interest those classes.

Programmes for Farmers.

Most important however in the domain of professional training are the programmes for farmers. They inform, instruct, advise and entertain peasants and all country dwellers who are often cut off from economic and cultural centres. In the United States particularly rural broadcasting has been greatly developed under the stimulus of the agricultural departments of the 48 States and of the agricultural colleges possessing their own transmitters. Private stations collaborate too—in July 1941 the Blue Network was able to send out over some hundred stations its 4000th "National Farm and Home Hour". A great effort is also made in certain of the Latin American countries, particularly in Cuba, where the government has created a special network of ten stations for the broadcasting of agricultural programmes.

Similarly the European radio services have greatly developed this type of work. In Italy, a special institution, "Ente Radio Rurale", carries on since 1933 an extensive activity which is both political and educational and which reaches country schools and the peasant population. In the Soviet Union the radio serves as the educator of peasants and the "kolkhozi" in order to secure improvement in agricultural methods. Many

---

[1] cf. Part A IV, p. 56.

other examples might be cited since a great many countries have today an excellent service which contributes to the raising of the economic and cultural standard of agricultural listeners [1].

The educational work of broadcasting in all its forms is of special value in countries where practical and scientific knowledge and above all knowledge of hygiene is by no means widespread. In vast regions of Latin America, China and India the radio station is often the sole educator—and an educator who is the better listened to that he speaks the language of natives who cannot read or write [2]. Already the educational work of broadcasting is no longer limited to national territories but carried out on the international and even on the intercontinental plane. The Columbia Broadcasting System has widened the framework of its American School of the Air which in 1940 became the "School of the Air of the Americas" (Radio Escuela de las Americas) and whose programmes were followed by 8 million children in the United States and 3 million in Canada and Latin America [3]. For years already the World Wide Broadcasting Foundation has transmitted over short waves educational programmes received by "students" in the five continents.

Religious Services.

In most countries religious broadcasts figure regularly on programmes. The proportion of time given to them varies considerably however : in 1939, it went from a few hours only on the French and Portuguese stations to 165 hours (2.1%) in Switzerland, 281 hours (6,3%) in Sweden and 420 hours

---

[1] One of the pioneer countries where agricultural radio is concerned was Czechoslovakia whose stations, in cooperation with the competent organizations, transmitted special daily programmes aiming both at the education of country folk and at the building up of contacts between town and country citizens as well as between different social classes.

[2] The South African Broadcasting Corporation has recently introduced transmissions in Zulu, Sotho and Rhosa, and the "All India Radio" in Hindustani, Tamil, Bengali, Marathi, Telugu, Gujarati, and Pushto.

[3] *Bulletin IBU,* September 1941, p. 301.

(about 10%) in Finland. The year 1940 has shown a considerable decrease of religious broadcasts in certain countries, such as Finland and Hungary, in others however, such as Italy and Danemark, a noteworthy increase. It should be remembered moreover that the majority of the listeners associations which were until 1940 responsible in Belgium and the Netherlands for a proportion of the programmes, were of a denominational character, and that in Australia, Uruguay, Venezuela and above all the United States there are radio stations owned and operated by religious institutions.

Programmes for the Forces.

War naturally influences the programmes, accentuating the political tendencies and multiplying the propaganda and news broadcasts. Moreover the predilections of soldiers play a dominant role in the composition of programmes. It is the "battle-front which inspires the programme content"—thus the Reich Minister of Propaganda [1]—and the front demands cheerful and restful broadcasts. The German stations take this into account in the general make-up of the programmes; the British stations have added to the ordinary broadcasts a "Programme for the Forces" (from 6.30 a.m. to 11.10 p.m.) which is for preference of a recreational nature ; the American, Japanese, and also Swiss and Swedish stations devote daily broadcasts to the army [2]. And in all the belligerent countries the radio serves as a link between the homes and the soldiers who are far away from their own country, transmitting every day numerous special broadcasts of news for the fighters and their families.

International Broadcasting.

International and intercontinental broadcasting developed parallel with the national service. It is served by a vast network of telephone circuits, high-power stations and above all by

---

[1] In an article published in the review *Das Reich* and broadcast by all German transmitters on June 14, 1941.

[2] Following a recent arrangement between the NBC and the U.S. Army, Navy and Marine Corps, the top-ranking programmes of the network are recorded and shortwaved around the globe for American servicemen abroad. *Broadcasting*, March 9, 1942.

the use of short waves. The exchange of programmes between countries and continents was stimulated by the wish to enrich broadcasts by picturesque and entertaining features and by the desire—sincere and genuine among broadcasters—for bringing people closer together. The International Broadcasting Union, acting as an intermediary between affiliated services, endeavoured to create and facilitate these exchanges and has since 1927 organized musical performances which each of its members agreed to relay. For their part the chief American companies appointed in 1930 European representatives responsible for arranging the transmission of any interesting programme [1]. Since then the international relays became more and more frequent : they numbered 447 in 1930, 1,079 four years later and 2,737 in 1937, not to mention the thousands of programmes regularly transmitted from Great Britain to various parts of the Empire, from the United States to Canada, from Japan to Manchukuo. In 1938 the CBS relayed 296 programmes from abroad, and the NBC even 578 coming from 49 countries. The interest in international programmes was so great that hundreds of stations often participated in the international relay arranged by the IBU of a musical festival or a national ceremony or event.

These exchanges continue, the belligerent countries of course excepted. The relays are just as numerous and even tend to increase owing to present events. In the first year of the war the NBC arranged 4,579 transmissions from Europe, of which 712 from England, 597 from Germany and 314 from France. In 1940 the BBC broadcast 426 foreign programmes, of which 101 from France, 92 from Egypt, 80 from the United States and some 20 from the Dutch East Indies. Furthermore seventeen countries relayed (between June 1940 and August 1941) 543 programmes from Germany, Brazil accounting for 102, Finland for 79, and Italy for 63 ; in addition, 1,572 news broadcasts were relayed by the stations of North America and 2,236 by those of South America [2].

---

[1] It is only in November 1941 that the radio relationship between the United States and Germany was interrupted by order of the German Government.

[2] cf. *Bulletin IBU*, September 1941, p. 293.

International relays are supplemented by programmes intended for listeners abroad. They are inspired on the one hand by the desire to strengthen the links with nationals living away from their own country and on the other by motives of political, economic, cultural or religious propaganda. Following the example of the powerful colonial station of Daventry and of the British Empire Service—inaugurated in 1932— important short-wave centres have been built for these ends. At the present time some thirty countries have organized special services which deal exclusively with international and intercontinental broadcasts.

This development is all the more amazing that international broadcasting has met with quite special difficulties : first of a financial order—it could not exact payment from listeners living abroad—secondly of a technical order, due to the over-crowding of frequency bands and the difference in time which makes it necessary to adopt a different hour of transmission for each zone and to repeat the same programme five or six times ; finally there are political, linguistic and psychological difficulties, since the broadcasts are intended for countries, nations and races of different structure and wholly different traditions. The national programmes had therefore to be carefully selected for short-wave transmission and when necessary adapted ; but experience has shown that in order to interest foreign listeners and exercise a lasting influence on them, it was indispensable to "build" special programmes, to broadcast them in the appropriate language and take into account preferences and individual interests. Hence this strange development of radio stations, whose words are most often incomprehensible to the inhabitants of the country itself.

In conformity with the aims which have governed this development the international programmes give pride of place to information. News best serves political propaganda and is most eagerly required by the distant listener. It was thus already in peace-time, and is even more so in time of war. But the artistic side is not excluded, for it also affords an excellent means of propaganda : to broadcast the literary and musical works is to excite the listener's interest in the national culture.

The Soviet Union was first to seize upon the possibilities of radio broadcasting for political propaganda and her example was soon imitated by Germany and Italy. Having within the country contributed to the victory of National-Socialism [1], the German radio was called upon to spread these ideas beyond the frontiers [2]. Already in 1935 the short-wave station sent out 25,697 transmissions; in the first year of the war 89,500 programmes were broadcast in thirty different languages and lasting a total of 35,500 hours [3]. And to the transmissions intended for other continents must be added those intended for Europe, broadcast in 27 languages and carried not only by the German stations but also by the powerful transmitters in the occupied countries [4], called today "Deutsche Europa-Sender" (German European Transmitters).

For a long time the democracies made no retort. "Radio-Colonial" was too weak to be heard even in all the French colonies; the British Broadcasting Corporation, though possessing an important short-wave centre, persisted in broadcasting only in English, while the Italian radio spoke already in 18 languages. It was only in 1938 that the BBC developed its international broadcasts, introducing in succession Arabic, Spanish and Portuguese programmes and finally German, Italian and French ones. In May 1942 the BBC Overseas Service, inheritor of the Empire Service, broadcast daily and during 24 hours on about forty short waves and five medium waves, hundreds of programmes and news bulletins in 39 languages : 30 in French, 19 in German, 10 in Italian and in Dutch, 8 in Czech and 7 in Polish, as well as a great number of Spanish and Portuguese broadcasts; there are even regular "news letters" for the Far East in ten Chinese and Indian languages and dialects. Political necessities also led the American broadcasters rapidly to develop their "international"

[1] Hitler has himself put it thus : "Ohne Kraftwagen, ohne Flugzeug und ohne Lautsprecher hätten wir Deutschland nicht erobert." (Without motor lorries, without aeroplanes and without loudspeakers we should not have conquered Germany). See *Handbuch des Deutschen Rundfunks*, 1938/39.

[2] As early as 1933 broadcasts in English were started.

[3] *cf. Weltrundfunk* 1941, No. 3 (June-July).

[4] Such as "Radio-Luxemburg", "Radio-Paris", Rennes, Bordeaux, Calais, Hilversum I, Prague, Dobrochau and Warsaw.

stations and programmes, directing them especially towards
Latin America and increasingly too towards Europe.

Today each short-wave service in the belligerent and neutral
countries broadcasts numerous news bulletins in foreign
languages. All means are used for the benefit of political
propaganda, so much so that at present almost all nations
are engaged in this war on waves. Thus broadcasting, created
to bring the peoples closer together has become, alas, a weapon
of war—the "fourth armament" [1].

The war has pitted the stations one against the other. But
it also strengthened the radio relationship between countries
that defend the same ideas and interests. This is shown by the
tightening of the links between the broadcasting services of the
British Empire. Even more significant is the recent development
of the *Pan-American broadcasting*—one of the most remarkable
facts in the history of the radio. How much ground has been
covered since that first concert of Latin American music given
on May 25, 1924 under the auspices of the Pan American
Union and transmitted from a studio in Washington ! Then
followed the dozens of relays of the Pan-American Conferences
at Montevideo in 1933 and Buenos Ayres in 1936. As a consequence of these meetings, which proclaimed the need of a close
collaboration of broadcasters between the two continents, the
NBC organized in 1937 its "International Division" and
inaugurated its transmissions in Spanish and Portuguese for
Latin America, soon followed by other American companies.
There was then initiated an intensive activity, encouraged by
the Government of the United States, the Pan American
Union and the Office of the Coordinator of Inter-American
Affairs (Rockefeller Committee), an activity extended and
re-enforced as political events in Europe promoted closer
relations between the American nations.

---

[1] We may mention here some special studies dealing with the
political aspects of radio : Thomas Grandin "The Political Use of
the Radio", *Geneva Studies* vol. X, No. 3, August 1939 ; John B.
Whitton, "War by Radio" in *Foreign Affairs*, April 1941, Harold
Graves, Jr. *War on the Short Waves*, Washington 1941 (Foreign
Policy Association, Headline Books No. 30) ; Claude Schubiger
La Guerre des Ondes, Lausanne 1941 ; Eckert "Der Rundfunk
als Führungsmittel" *Studien zum Weltrundfunk*, vol. I, Heidelberg
1941 ; Charles J. Rolo, *Radio goes to War*, New York 1942.

The short-wave frequencies reserved for Pan-American broadcasting [1] have been given to the "international" stations, who were obliged to increase their power to a minimum of 50 kW. Parallel with this, transmissions for Latin America greatly increased, giving for preference popular music or dealing with questions of interest to the Western Hemisphere. From 1936 to 1937 the number of programmes built up specially by the NBC and transmitted by its Bound Brook station rose from 184 to 3,179 ; to the languages spoken by the Latin American peoples were soon added English and the languages of the emigrant populations, Italian, German, and French. At present, the international stations of the USA carry on a service of 20 hours and more, as much to Europe as to Latin America ; some stations speak in 16 or even 22 languages.

For years the American companies themselves bore the cost of this strictly non-commercial service, without any hope of covering their ever-growing expenses. It was only in December 1939 that the government authorized the broadcasting of commercial programmes in order to extend the field of activity and stimulate the inter-American economic relationships. The addition of new capital provided by the advertisers gave a new impulse to this activity, allowing it to offer listeners the best programmes of the United States—Toscanini concerts, performances at the Metropolitan Opera or revues with the most famous stars of Hollywood. Industrial, commercial and tourist concerns, specially interested in relations with Latin America, finance weekly and even daily series of programmes ; some of them broadcast on their own account the news bulletins of the big American press agencies.

In addition to this great cultural efforts are made, as witness to which may be taken the high number of educational broadcasts which tend to promote feeling for a Pan-American community.

To ensure the reception of their programmes and to control their results, the heads of the NBC, the CBS and the Crosley Corporation, accompanied by a staff of engineers and other radio experts, visited the Latin American republics in the summer of 1941. There was then decided the formation of

---

[1] 6120-9559-11,730-15,130 and 21,500 kilocycles.

the Latin American networks, mentionned above, which include hundreds of stations and rebroadcast daily programmes of the United States.

It goes without saying that the Latin American services do not only agree to "receive", but wish also to "give". Many of them today make considerable efforts to arrange programmes which might interest listeners in the United States and might be incorporated in the programmes of the American networks. At the same time, the government of Brazil, following the example of the American advertisers, buys time from the USA stations in order to make national, economic and tourist propaganda.

The development of Pan-American broadcasting though it is only in its beginnings, meets the wishes of listeners in all parts of the continent. On both sides a warm welcome is given to programmes and this stimulates cultural and economic relations between the two Americas.

IV. RECEPTION

Even as for transmission, so for listening, there are two different aspects : direct reception and indirect reception. The first is by radio, from the station to the receiver ; the second by wire, through the intermediary of a central receiving station or another service of programme distribution. In the one case the listener is free to choose among the broadcasts that he can get and compose "his" programme by going from station to station ; in the other he must be content with the choice of broadcasts selected for him amongst the national programmes and several foreign programmes.

Individual and Collective Listening.

There is yet another division to be made according to the manner of listening—individual or collective. Favoured for political or educational reasons, the latter has developed rapidly. In all countries with a dictatorial regime governments see to it that their broadcasts, intended for the masses, reach the greatest possible number of listeners ; loud-speakers are placed in the streets and on public squares, in work-rooms and recreation halls. In the Soviet Union wire broadcasting and group listening are closely allied, the factories, clubs, libraries, kolkhoz and other meeting places being linked to a central receiving station. Moreover an educational broadcast gains in value if it can be immediately commented and discussed ; group listening is also applied in school broadcasting, the agricultural radio and finally the workers radio. Following the example given in 1927 by the BBC "listening circles" have been formed in numerous countries ; there are in Great Britain some 800 "discussion groups" over 1,000 in Sweden and in Finland, and in the United States even 15,000 with about 500,000 members [1]. In that country, listeners also take an active part in the public debates frequently organized by American stations [2].

Common interests unite the users. Amateurs·with special technical interests constitute radio clubs ; listeners, who are devotees of the radio and desire to be present at a transmission in the studio itself collect together in big associations, the chief of which had before the war over 100,000 members. Sometimes the listeners thus grouped could send delegates to represent them in the governing bodies and the advisory committees of the broadcasting organizations [3].

Listeners' Collaboration and Influence.

The participation of listeners in the concerns of the radio is also manifested in other ways. Of these correspondence is the most popular : every day thousands of listeners write to the broadcast services to put forward their requests and criticisms, propose changes and suggest new ideas. Thus in 1941 the NBC had received 6,750,000 letters ; that means that 18,493 persons write every day in the year. Often the services have special departments to sort and analyse the letters, to

---

[1] Results of a study conducted in 1941 by Ernest Hill for the American Association for Adult Education.

[2] See Arthur Garfield Hays "Civic Discussion Over the Air", in *The Annals*, January 1941, pp. 37-46.

[3] Until 1939 listeners in France, in Belgium, in Denmark and especially in the Netherlands had a real influence on the management of the stations and the composition of programmes.

answer questions and maintain friendly relations with the public. Often too, letters are published in the official radio magazines—the listeners thus have a "platform"—or letters which have a general interest are discussed at the microphone.

More instructive even are the inquiries, general or special, the results of which reveal how the audience is made up, what its reactions and preferences are. Most important of these are the investigations carried out on behalf of the big American companies, solicitous of controlling the effect of their advertising programmes ; then the inquiry undertaken in 1931 by the former Austrian society (the RAVAG) and quite recently the big "Referendum" of the EIAR, the Italian radio organization which has collected very detailed answers from 901,386 owners of sets, i.e. 75% of the total number of its subscribers [1].

Without always following the wishes of the public—sometimes that would be disastrous—broadcasters have many opportunities of easily falling in with the suggestions and wishes of the listeners, by getting a better balance for instance between certain types of programme, by including the lectures asked for or by changing the hour of a broadcast.

Another way of interesting listeners in the radio is the competition which sometimes calls upon their creative powers, sometimes upon their powers of criticism or their memory. These competitions, often rewarded by substantial prizes, are very popular and have often a great many entries. Moreover, the radio services have thus discovered many new collaborators : composers, writers, artists, commentators and speakers.

The right and influence of listeners largely depend on the radio system which conditions the attitude of broadcasters towards the public.

For the private radio the listener is the law ; every effort is made for him and he is offered all that he desires without paying a cent. Proudly the broadcasters of the United States declare : "American radio is free. It gives the right to listen and the right to be heard... No censor tells us what we *shall*

---

[1] The analysis of these answers has shown, with all the precision that may be desired, the reactions of Italian listeners. Like the inquiry of the RAVAG it revealed the astonishing lack of interest in sporting broadcasts demanded only by 4,093 listeners and refused by the majority. *Cf.* "Referendum EIAR", publication of results of the inquiry, Turin 1940.

.hear and what we *shall not* hear" [1]. For the official radio the
listeners is a "vassal", obliged to pay for the right to listen ;
but far from dictating his wishes to the director of the service,
he is the "pupil" of the government, his "master". In the
authoritarian countries the state does not only impose broadcasts of a certain character, but assumes the right to forbid
the reception of foreign programmes. The example was given
by Germany where, already long before the war, listening
in to the Soviet stations was severely punished. Since the
beginning of war this measures has been extended to all
foreign broadcasts [2].

Needless to say these measures limit listening in to the
radio whose freedom was its greatest privilege as well as one
of its main attractions. But in spite of the risks run by those
who disobey, the prohibition does not wholly remove foreign
influence. After the war the extent of clandestine listening
will be revealed ; there is plenty of evidence which allows one
to conclude that propaganda broadcasts are to a certain
extent efficacious [3].

Number and Density of "Radio Homes" [4].

In spite of restrictions and of the obstacles due to the present
political situation—not the least of these are the shortage of raw
materials necessary for the radio industry, and the difficulties
of international trade—the number of receivers ceaselessly
increases from year to year, even from month to month.

---

[1] *Cf. The ABC of Radio* ; National Association of Broadcasters,
Washington 1938.

[2] This prohibition is also valid for foreigners living in German
or occupied territory ; they are thus deprived of links with their
own country, even if it is a neutral one. (*Cf. Deutsche Justiz*,
1940, No. 14 and *Rundfunkarchiv*, Berlin, October and November
1939, January 1940).

[3] For instance : letters which have reached the American radio
services from the occupied zones ; mass confiscations of receivers ;
the increasing number of sentences on listeners "guilty" of having
listened to foreign broadcasts ; the increasing severity of penalties
—hard labour and even death penalty.

[4] The term "density" is used to denote the proportion of homes
equipped with radio receivers per thousand inhabitants.

This continuous growth of the audience is the surest sign of the progress and the importance of radio broadcasting.

At the beginning of 1936, according to licences and reliable estimates, 56,764,628 receivers were in use, and in January 1941 nearly 120 million. The number of *radio homes* was about 96,106,000 divided as follows in the various continents [1] :

North and Central America	31,864,000
South America	2,028,000
Europe (including the U.S.S.R. and Turkey) .	51,986,000
Asia	7,968,000
Oceania	1,653,000
Africa	607,000
Total	96,106,000

The United States were at the head with 29,397,000 "radio homes". 11,000,000 Americans were no longer content with one apparatus, but owned two or even three ; there were counted also 1,800,000 portable receivers and no less than 8,000,000 "auto-sets" [2]. The total was of receivers number about 52 million.

Germany followed with 14,965,048 licences, the Soviet Union with 10,551,361 licences [3] and Great Britain with 9,132,200 licences [3] ; then Japan with 5,369,898, France with 5,133,035 and China with about 2,000,000 receivers. Canada had 1,676,530 licences, Sweden 1,470,375, the Netherlands 1,440,626, Italy 1,400,000, Australia 1,212,581 [4] and Belgium 1,102,130. The Argentine and Poland had also passed the first million, Denmark, Bohemia and Moravia are nearing that figure.

New statistics are not yet available for all countries ; we may quote however some figures for the beginning of 1942 :

---

[1] Figures based on diagrams and the information of the International Broadcasting Office, Geneva ; the *Broadcasting Yearbook*, 1941 ; documents of the FCC, and the U.S. Department of Commerce, Washington ; official reports of the broadcasting organizations.

[2] Estimates of the well-known American expert Dr. O. H. Caldwell, also adopted in the official statistics of the FCC.

[3] End September 1940.

[4] End June 1940.

30,300,000 radio homes and a total of 57,400,000 receivers for the United States ; 15,843,144 licences for Germany, including all the incorporated territories ; 8,625,579 for Great Britain and 5,262,642 for France ; 1,674,546 are counted in Italy, 1,550,691 in Sweden and 1,431,791 in the Netherlands,

Almost all radio listeners use direct reception. In one country alone, the U.S.S.R., the majority is served by wire ; according to official information dating from the end of 1940 the relay exchanges provided more than 6,000,000 reception posts with programmes. The 800 relay exchanges of the Netherlands had 255,000 subscribers, the wire broadcast services in Great Britain over 250,000 and those of Switzerland 93,000. There are some thousands of subscribers in Germany, in Belgium and in Hungary and a few hundred in the British and Dutch colonies, especially in Nigeria and the Gold Coast, the Falkland Islands and Curaçao.

The importance of broadcasting in a country is shown not only by the number of receivers, but even more so by the number of homesteads equipped with receivers as compared with the number of inhabitants [1]. Estimated thus the order of countries is considerably altered. At the beginning of 1942, Sweden comes first with 243.40 licences per thousand inhabitants, followed by Denmark with 233.91°/$_{oo}$—a radio country if ever there was one and which from 1922 to 1936 held the first place—and then only come the United States of America with more then 230 per thousand. New Zealand with 212.10 licences and Great Britain with 187.51 rank in front of Germany which in spite of the very high figure for licences, has only 177.48 sets per thousand inhabitants [2]. And many small countries—Iceland (170.69), Switzerland (159.84), the Netherlands (159.09), Norway (145.46)[3] and Belgium (136.20)[3]—come before France which only has 125.60 per thousand, the Soviet Union (62.07), Italy (36.90) and Spain (11.15). But the example of the United States and of the Scandinavian countries shows that it is possible to reach the ideal aim of the radio : "a receiver

---

[1] See Annex II.

[2] In the original territory of the Reich (Altreich), however, the density is much higher.

[3] January 1941.

in each home". In order to get the number of *listeners*, one must in general count four persons per set ; in several countries however such as Mexico, Japan, China, Italy and the Soviet Union the proportion is far higher owing to large families or because of the practice of collective listening.

The audience is further increased by several millions of clandestine listeners ; it is a fact that many people omit—through negligence, ill-will, or through a spirit of opposition—to declare their receivers, especially in the countries where these are liable to taxes [1]. Experience has shown in France, in Great Britain, in India and in New Zealand that the number of declarations rises suddenly each time that a severe drive is launched against clandestine listeners, threatening them with more or less heavy fines. On the other hand the Spanish authorities take few appropriate measures, since they consider "that in the present circumstances a large number of unregistered listeners is preferable to a smaller number of legal licence-holders" [2].

Similarly several Latin American governments have given up the collection of taxes—even the taxes themselves—since it was impossible to collect them without devoting to the controlling services sums far higher than would have been brought in by the licence fees.

Taking it all in all, we may estimate, without too great a margin of error, that the radio public consists of more than 400,000,000 listeners. A short while ago the most optimistic of the experts had fixed the saturation point at 100,000,000 receivers. But even though today it has been exceeded, the number of receivers yet steadily increases by ten millions a year, that is by 40-50 million listeners. For though the limit will soon be reached in some countries, there are still vast regions, especially in Asia, Africa, and Latin America, where a receiver is a luxury reserved for the wealthier classes. The interest however in contemporary political events and the need for speedy information bring the radio many new listeners every day.

---

[1] In Brazil for instance when the authorities required a tax, 4,000 receivers were registered out of the 175,000 in use.
[2] *Bulletin IBU*, July 1941, p. 235.

The role played by broadcasting at the present time is clearly illustrated when we compare the figures for receivers with those for newspaper circulation ; in 1940 the 814 stations of the United States served 50,100,000 receivers, whereas the total circulation of the 1,877 American dailies was only of 41,009,258 copies [1]. The radio is thus able even better than the press to reach the entire nation. That is particularly the case on the occasion of significant political events : one of the recent addresses of President Roosevelt, broadcast on February 23, 1942, over the major networks and by numerous independent stations, was heard by 80 to 83% of all the set owners in the United States, that is an average audience of about 62,000,000 adult listeners [2] ; moreover it was broadcast simultaneously by the international stations of the country and relayed by 211 stations of Latin America and those of Canada and Great Britain.

* * *

400 million people are listening in. Thus 20 years have given broadcasting a big place in the life of today. And its sphere of action is not limited to the radio services, but extends to the economic and social domains. With enormous financial means at its disposal, it controls an enormous turnover of capital and exerts a constant influence on numerous industrial and commercial activities. First of all the national economy has increased its revenues through payments, taxes and duties levied on broadcasters. Similarly private enterprise has greatly benefited from the radio's needs of all kinds of material, varying from machinery and cables to scores and musical instruments.

Broadcasting has given birth to important branches of the radio industry and trade. The manufacture and sale of radio material represents enormous sums and nothing better illustrates the economic importance of broadcasting than the value

---

[1] *Cf. Editor and Publisher* Yearbooks. See also Annex III.

[2] Result of detailed inquiries by the Cooperative Analysis of Broadcasting (CAB) and C.E. Hooper, Inc., *cf. Broadcasting*, March 9, 1942, p. 35.

of receivers. The 52 million receivers used in 1941 in the United States represent a capital of $3,200,000,000 and further necessitate an annual expenditure of $220,000,000 [1] ; but broadcasting is also useful to other industries, especially the telephone, owing to the intensive use of lines and circuits [2].

Another example of the economic repercussions of broadcasting is that of the consumption of electric power. According to the statistics for 1939, the world's transmitters, then of a total power of 19,079 kilowatts required 516,200,000 kWh, a figure increased by 50 to 80% by the needs of studios ; the receivers, then numbering 89,900,000, used 4,507,500,000 kWh ; the radio electrical industry required 400 millions and the radio trade a further 100 millions of kWh [3]. Thus the broadcasting activity of the world had led to an annual consumption of 5 to 6,000,000,000 of kilowatt-hours, the cost [4] of which was 1,500,000,000 Swiss francs.

As many examples show, radio advertising has an unquestionable influence on business. The time for transmission, often so dearly bought, brings profit to the advertisers by considerably increasing the sales. For the appeal of the living voice makes the publicity convincing ; it influences moreover a public which listens regularly to the programmes it likes. Listening in to commercial broadcasts creates new customers. The 40 programmes broadcast in January 1940 by the CBS recruited 37 million more users and buyers for the advertised products ; a single programme increased the number of users of one product by as much as 4,400,000 [5]. In every case the number of "product-users" was higher among the listeners than among those who do not hear the programme. All investigations reach the same conclusion : "public listens, then buys".

---

[1] Estimates of Dr. O.H. Caldwell, *cf. Broadcasting* December 15, 1941.

[2] For instance 6,000 miles of special telephone lines link up the transmitters and studios of the BBC.

[3] *Cf. Bulletin IBU*, October 1940, study of Raymond Braillard, based on the results of an inquiry undertaken by the Union.

[4] Calculated at the medium rate of 10 centimes for the stations and commercial usage, and of 30 centimes for the receivers.

[5] *Cf. Roper Counts Customers*, results of a nationwide inquiry undertaken by Elmo Roper : Columbia Broadcasting System, New York 1941.

It has also been proved that repeated listening to a certain programme increases the sales figures : "The more they listen, the more they buy" [1]. The success of commercial broadcasts explains the constant progress of radio advertising, preferred more and more by big commercial firms ; in 1940 the sale of time on the national networks of the NBC, CBS and MBS exceeded by 8 million dollar the sale of space in the daily newspapers, and by 15 million dollars that in reviews and magazines [2].

Finally broadcasting gives work to an army of technicians and artists. It has caused new professions to arise, ranging from that of the radio engineer to speaker ; the best artistic talents is indebted to it, and innumerable artists, lecturers, reporters and other occasional collaborators earn their daily bread through it. In 1941 more than 250,000 persons were employed in the radio industry of the United States excluding part-time employees and artists ; their pay roll exceeded $350,000 [3]. And if one takes into account the personnel of the broadcasting services, of the radio manufacturing and commercial firms in other countries, it is no exaggeration to say that millions of men live thanks to radio broadcasting.

---

[1] Results of five inquiries carried out from 1939 to 1941 by C.E. Hooper for the NBC.

[2] Analysis issued by the NBC Research Division ; cf. *Broadcasting*, July 21, 1941.

[3] Figures given by the NBC, New York 1942.

B. RADIO BROADCASTING
IN THE VARIOUS COUNTRIES

The radio wears different aspects in each continent and in the different countries. The influence of the national character and of the political "regime" is reflected in each system, in the structure of the services and in the composition of the programmes.

During the past few years the situation has changed profoundly, these changes being due to technical progress, to economic and social fluctuations, and largely to the effects of armed conflict. Certain countries which until 1934 and even 1936 were very much behind the general development of the radio have suddenly begun to improve their services. Hence the extraordinary impulse manifested in the British Empire and more recently in Latin America. On the other hand political crises, both internal and foreign, have long delayed progress in Spain and in the Balkan countries. But no event has had more serious consequences than the war in Europe and in Asia which has upset the radio situation in these continents.

I. EUROPE

Europe is the present-day centre of radio activity. Its influence is felt in the most isolated regions of other continents. It is from Daventry that originate many programmes broadcast daily in the Falkland Islands, in Newfoundland or in the heart of Africa ; it is from Zeesen that is spread the National-Socialist propaganda and from the Vatican City that sound the peace-making words of the Pope. The whole world listens to Europe.

Many years had to pass before the European radio was able to overcome hindrances and difficulties which up to a point still remain today. For the problems which also arise in other continents are here made more serious by the infinitely

smaller space available—the cause of interference and un-
welcome influences—by the profound national differences and
the multitude of languages. Before the war the variety of radio
services and systems corresponded to this multi-coloured
variety of nations and national interests. Every kind of radio
regime was current, from the commercial station, broadcasting
advertising matter from morning till night, to the government station wholly at the political service of the party in
power. Since then the structure of the European radio has
been greatly "simplified"—broadcasting organizations have
been dissolved, numerous services suppressed or taken over
by the government. The war has put an end to the successful
development of the radio in Czechoslovakia, in Poland and
in the Baltic states ; it has seriously affected French broadcasting and upset the system in the Netherlands, in Belgium,
in Luxemburg and in Jugoslavia [1]. Everywhere, even in the
countries that have hitherto been spared war, official control
has been tangibly strengthened, especially for political and
news broadcasts. Yet a certain diversity still obtains—
contrarily to what is believed and often stated in print outside
Europe. Broadcasting organization, choice of programmes
and the listeners' rights fully illustrate this, especially in the
two countries whose services dominate Europe : Great Britain
and Germany.

Great Britain

Great Britain has from the beginning played an extremely
important role in the development of the radio. It was the
first to set up a proper broadcasting system and its experience
has served as an example for many countries ; its organization has been taken as a model even as its conception of
broadcasting as a "public service". Always financed by a
licence fee, the society could wholly abstain from sale of time

---

[1] It is impossible to predict how far these changes will be
permanent—they certainly cannot all be so, for each radio system,
set up after various trials and modifications, more or less answered
to the conditions and the needs of these countries. It is for this
reason that we consider it necessary to mention in the following
pages the original system before analyzing that of today.

for commercial programmes. Yet it was never a government department ; though officially controlled and responsible to Parliament, the radio has enjoyed even at times of crisis a large measure of independence and was managed in the spirit of the British liberal tradition.

"Acting as Trustees for the national interest", the *British Broadcasting Corporation (BBC)* is in charge of the service for Great Britain and Northern Ireland. It functions as a public corporation by virtue of a Royal Charter [1] and a licence granted for ten years by the Postmaster General. In normal times the latter alone supervises the service, but since September 1939 he shares this right with the Minister of Information [2]. But still today the BBC has a considerable autonomy : it builds and operates the stations, it is responsible for its own administration, and for the programme service, broadcasts of a political character excepted [3]. The Charter has been maintained in its integrity and the restrictions imposed for reasons of national defence are, as has been stated by the government itself, only of a provisional nature.

The Corporation is directed by a Board of Governors, distinguished personalities appointed by the King in Council. The executive functions are fulfilled by a Director-General, a Deputy Director-General and the "Controllers" of the chief divisions [4]. In peace time some twenty advisory councils and committees assisted the BBC in its difficult and complex task. For pratical reasons only six have been retained, charged with special questions such as musical programmes, school broadcasting, religious services and appeals on behalf of charities. On the other hand many broadcasters, representing the radio

---

[1] Dated January 1, 1927 and renewed January 1, 1937.

[2] The powers relating mainly to technical matters remain with the Postmaster General ; other powers, mainly relating to programme matters, hours of broadcasting and the possible control of the service in emergency, were transferred to the Minister of Information. *Cf.: BBC Handbook* 1941, p. 111.

[3] The political and news broadcasts are controlled either by the Ministry of Information or a special committee, the Political Warfare Executive.

[4] For the duration of the war the duties of the Director-General have been entrusted in January 1942 to wo Directors-General, the one responsible for the general production policy, the other for the business side.

organizations of the Empire, actively collaborate with the BBC especially in the programmes for the Dominions.

Today the service consists of six "Divisions"—each grouping several departments, and further sub-divided when necessary— Administration, Finance, Engineering, the "Programme Division", responsible for most programmes ; information and lectures, however, fall to the "Home Division", and the overseas broadcasts to the "Overseas Division" where are centralized all services working for the Empire and foreign countries.

The licence fee, permanently fixed at 10 shillings per annum and actually yielding about £4,500,000, is the chief source of income of the Corporation; for a long time however the BBC only received a limited part of this revenue [1] but the Corporation's share has been raised year by year in order to allow it to fulfil multifarious new tasks. The revenue is also considerably increased because the BBC acts as its own publisher and issues several important radio weeklies, dozens of booklets relating to programmes, bulletins, handbooks and annuals.

The British network, one of the best organized in the world, provided in peace time a number of alternative services for the entire territory of the United Kingdom. Four stations, among them the 150 kW long wave transmitter at Droitwich broadcast the "national programme", while twelve others, mostly of 70 to 100 kW, sent out the various "regional programmes". To these were added the transmissions for the Empire, broadcast by the six short-wave transmitters of the colonial centre at Daventry of 10 to 50 kW, and the daily television programmes, carried out until the beginning of the war through an important station in London [2]. This service has been modified in conformity with the needs of war, and consists today of three distinct groups : the "Home Service", a single programme for listeners in Great Britain ; the "Programme

---

[1] Until 1936 the Corporation received 90% of the sum collected on the first million licences, 80% on the second million, 70% on the third, and 60% on the following ; the new Charter granted it, after deduction of the Post Office expenses in the collection of taxes, a minimum of 75%, this sum being increased by 8% in 1937/38 and by 15% in 1938/39. Since then, in accordance with an agreement concluded between the Minister of Information and the Treasury, it receives the sums that it needs.

[2] See part C, p. 150.

for the Forces", inaugurated on January 7, 1940 and intended for British troops abroad ; finally, the "Overseas Services", subdivided into four sections according to their tasks : Empire, European, North American and Latin American Services.

The number of wave lengths used in the Home Service has been considerably reduced for military reasons [1], the number of stations and their power greatly increased in order to extend the reach of transmissions. Precise details are not published, but it is known that several powerful transmitters have been built since the outbreak of the war in closely-guarded secret places, ready for immediate service, should one of the ordinary stations be put out of action. It has thus been possible to ensure the continuous broadcasting of programmes even in heavily bombarded regions [2]. At the same time, the "Overseas Transmitters" have been brought up to 100 kW—perhaps even more—and now use some forty frequencies so that at least some of their broadcasts may be heard in spite of the violent jamming by enemy stations. Since the beginning of the war, numerous services have been moved to the provinces ; but notwithstanding the bombardments and the serious damage caused to Broadcasting House in London, the work has never stopped there ; in the underground studios beds have been put up next to the microphones and first aid stations next to the engineer's control board [3].

The maxim "Tolerate everything that is tolerable" has always ruled the British programmes which aimed at conciliating all the trends of public life, the traditions, the habits and the tastes of the various peoples in the United Kingdom. Often the different aspects of a problem were put forward during debates. At election time, the representatives of the chief political parties were able to state their case on the microphone. The BBC has endeavoured, by reports and relays from abroad, to inform the listeners as to happenings outside their country and has set forth the political structure, the

---

[1] The wave length which reveals the location of a station may give precious information to enemy aircraft.

[2] *Cf.* statement of Mr. William M. Newton, member of the BBC's New York staff, in *Broadcasting*, June 2, 1941, p. 14.

[3] *Ibidem.*

economic, social and educational experience of other countries, whether democratic or totalitarian. The present situation has necessarily modified this liberal policy, obliging the BBC in the first instance to serve government policy and national propaganda.

Present-day interests and consequently news broadcasts predominate in the programmes, especially in those intended for abroad. At the outbreak of the war, the BBC broadcast weekly 44 hours of programmes in foreign languages—at the end of 1941 there were 50-60 hours every day with an unbroken chain of news bulletins in 39 languages. And these activities are constantly being expanded. But the artistic and educational side has at no time been neglected, especially where school broadcasting, most carefully tended in Great Britain, is concerned ; after a temporary uncertainty, the programmes began once more to develop and improve. Moreover listening to foreign stations was never forbidden : the British listener can freely choose between the stations of New York and Moscow or those of Berlin and Rome[1].

Until 1936 Great Britain had, among the European countries, the highest number of listeners. Today it still keeps the third place with nearly 9 million licences and 187.51 sets per thousand inhabitants. And the audience of BBC programmes is greatly increased thanks to the daily relays by the stations of the whole British Empire.

Germany
(including the Incorporated and Occupied Territories).

The German radio regime is in complete contrast, and not only since the war, with the British system : it is one of official ownership and operation, based on the authoritarian principle. That same system has been imposed upon the countries which have now passed under the domination of the Reich, in so far as the German authorities have allowed them to retain a broadcasting organization.

Even at the time when the German radio was run by some ten private and regional societies, affiliated to the *Reichs-Rundfunk-Gesellschaft (RRG)*, the government of the Reich

---

[1] A radio review even publishes a monthly list of foreign stations broadcasting news in English.

and of the federated states controlled and influenced the programmes, delegating commissioners and counsellors to the boards of directors and advisory committees. The advent of National-Socialism, in the spring of 1933, consummated that slow development towards state control by overthrowing the existing system : the radio societies were abolished and incorporated into the RRG, which then became an official institution ; and all the stations were placed under the direct control of the state and the National-Socialist party. Henceforth the service "has purely political functions... even its cultural, entertainment and current history broadcasts serve a higher political order..." [1].

The supreme head of the German radio is the "Reichspropagandaminister" who is at the same time the "Reichspropagandaleiter" of the National-Socialist party. Unity of direction from the state and the party is ensured by the fact that the head of a government service is also the holder of the corresponding post in the party.

The section "Broadcasting" of the Reichsministerium für Volksaufklärung und Propaganda is so to speak the "G.H.Q." (Befehlszentrale) of the German radio. Orders are sent out from there to the executive, the *Reichs-Rundfunk-Gesellschaft* which runs the whole service, with the exception of the building and technical operation of the transmitters, of which the Reichspost ministry is in charge. Constituted as a joint-stock company, the RRG is in reality a state service, since it is the state that holds all the shares ; and government representatives preside over the Board of Directors and the Supervisory Council.

At the head of the broadcasting service is a "Reichsintendant" who is also the Director-General of the RRG. He has under his orders the chiefs of the three divisions : Administration, Engineering and Programmes (Reichssendeleitung-Programmdirektion) and the directors of the principal stations, who have the title of "Intendant". Under the orders of the

---

[1] "Der deutsche Rundfunk hat rein politische Funktionen... selbst seine kulturellen, unterhaltenden und das Zeitgeschehen gestaltenden Sendungen dienen einer höheren politischen Ordnung..." Hans Kriegler, "Der deutsche Rundfunk — Aufgabe und Organisation", in the *Handbuch des Deutschen Rundfunks*, 1938/9, pp. 7-12.

"Intendants" work the chiefs of the parallel sections (administration, engineering, programmes) and the directors of the local stations in their respective regions. There is no advisory council or committee whatsoever ; formerly these were numerous. An important and special feature of the German organization is the strict application of the principle of a division of labour between the departments in charge of the planning of programmes and those responsible for their execution [1].

Like other government services, the broadcasting society is annually financed by the government, which collects a very high licence fee from owners of sets ; it is of 24 marks a year and brings in at present 360 million marks, used not only to cover the expenses of the radio services, but also to subsidize theatres and orchestras, schools in the frontier regions and popular libraries [2].

The network of the Reich is made up of a powerful long-wave station, the "Deutschlandsender" of 150 kW, of central stations in the various regions—called "Reichssender" and generally of 100 or 120 kW—and of local stations with 0,5 to 5 kW, affiliated to the central stations. There is besides at Zeesen the great short-wave centre, (with transmitters of 12, 20 or 50 kW) and a television station in the capital. Comprising in 1937 twenty-six stations—ten high-powered and sixteen relay-stations—the German network has been greatly enlarged owing to political events. When a new territory came under the authority of the Reich, the stations of these regions were immediately incorporated in the RRG, the main station as a "Reichssender" (or as "Landessender") and the others as relay stations of a central transmitter. Consequently, the German programmes are now broadcast by 128 transmitters [3], such as the powerful long-wave stations "Radio-Paris", Hilversum I ("Friesland"), Luxemburg, Warsaw I ("Weichsel") and Oslo, as well as twenty-two short-wave transmitters, among them "Paris-Mondial", Huizen, and Podiebrad.

---

[1] *Cf.* the articles of the Reichsintendant Dr. Heinrich Glasmeier, "Die Reichs-Rundfunk-G.m.b.H." and "Die Neuordnung des Grossdeutschen Rundfunks", in the *Handbuch des Deutschen Rundfunks*", 1938/39, pp. 18-20 and 1939/40, pp. 16-20.

[2] H.J. Weinbrenner "Die Grundelemente des Rundfunks", *Handbuch des Deutschen Rundfunks*, 1939/40, p. 23.

[3] *Cf. Rundfunkarchiv*, April 1942.

The centre of this vast activity is the "Funkhaus" in Berlin, the headquarters of the RRG which owns other buildings in the big provincial towns and in Vienna, and besides uses the premises and studios in the occupied territories.

Broadcasting and National-Socialism are one. Broadcasting, described by one of the heads of the German radio as a means of "psychological infection" [1], acts as the voice of the party and of the political leaders. Definite propaganda programmes apart, everything else serves propaganda too.

Thus the political element predominates in the programme. The main broadcasts consist of the speeches of the leaders and of running commentaries. In 1939 thirteen German stations reserved no less than 19,096 hours to information and in 1940 more than 30,000 hours, without including the lectures, radio plays and broadcasts for the young, all of which derive their inspiration from political and contemporary themes. Of course the propaganda also aims at reaching listeners abroad ; much political matter is broadcast for them in 27 languages.

In contrast with "political centralization", there is "cultural decentralization" which takes into account the varying German provinces and the regions placed under the authority of the Reich. Each group of stations endeavours to reflect by the transmission of numerous regional and local programmes the special character of each district, its traditions, its customs, its folklore, its art. Regular exchanges of programmes, in accordance with a methodical plan ensuring the collaboration of all the transmitters, help the population of one province to get to know the characteristics of others. Moreover the work of each transmitter is thus reduced, the means available for various programmes are increased and listeners are offered a fairly rich choice of programmes [2].

Before the war there were up to thirteen different programmes ; but the service has since been seriously reduced and

---

[1] See the article of Regierungsrat H.J. Weinbrenner quoted above.

[2] In 1938 the stations of the Reich exchanged among themselves 52.7% of news broadcasts, 48.4% of musical programmes, 14.9% of lectures, and 11% of literary broadcasts. *Cf. Handbuch des Deutschen Rundfunks*, 1939/40, pp. 320-322.

is limited [1] to one general programme ; two programmes are broadcast only in the main listening hours (and only since March 1, 1942) : the one by all the Reichssender giving light entertainment, the other by the Deutschlandsender offering more serious entertainment such as operas and symphonic concerts ; in addition, there are the programmes intended for European and over-seas listeners, broadcast on long and short waves.

Government activity is duplicated by that of the National-Socialist party and its radio section [2], which has regional and branch offices in all the provinces and districts. The heads of these offices, acting as political and radio propagandists, set up community receivers, distribute thousands of sets and serve as intermediaries between the broadcast service and the people [3]. This propaganda activity is also seconded by the radio industry which, at the request of the Minister for Propaganda, manufactures cheap sets called "Volksempfänger", the introduction of which has increased the number of receivers by several millions [4]. Finally, in order to bring broadcasting to the poor, the authorities issue hundreds of thousands of free licences (about 1,200,000 at present). Reception is "organized" and collective listening is practised on a large scale ; in the hotels, restaurants and cafés absolute silence is ordered at the time of the news bulletins [5] ; the reception of news bulletins is compulsory even in the upper school classes during lesson time [6]. With the obligation to listen to the German

---

[1] According to the information given by the German press.

[2] Amtsleitung "Rundfunk" der Reichspropagandaleitung der NSDAP.

[3] For many years another official institution concerned itself with radio questions, the Reichs-Rundfunkkammer, whose special task was to watch over the interests of German broadcasters and to promote propaganda for the radio ; it was dissolved on October 28, 1939 and its rights and obligations were transferred to the RRG.

[4] Propaganda for the radio was also furthered by some thirty programme magazines, the chief of which had in 1939 a circulation of 1,200,000 copies ; they were all suppressed however on May 31, 1941 in order to free people and material for other important war purposes ("um Menschen und Material für andere kriegswichtige Zwecke freizumachen").

[5] Bulletin IBU, March 1941, p. 79.

[6] Ordinance of the Regierungspräsident at Munich. Cf. "Der Schweizerische Rundspruch", No. 13, December 12, 1940.

broadcasts goes the prohibition of listening to foreign stations [1].
All infringement of these orders is considered as a "Rundfunk-
verbrechen" (radio crime) punished often by hard labour
during four to six years or even by the death penalty [2].
As does the great number of stations controlled by the
Reich, so too the number of receivers—16 million in the spring
of 1942—shows the scope and the influence of the German
radio.

* * *

In the territories incorporated in the Reich or occupied by
its armies, the broadcasting services were in part suppressed
and their stations simply annexed [3]. Such was the fate of the
stations of Saarbrücken, Danzig, and Memel as well as of
the Austrian network, run since 1924 by the *Oesterreichische
Radio Verkehrs A. G.* (RAVAG), a limited company but closely
linked with the government ; the "Ostmark" gave the Reich
nine stations, of which that of Vienna-Bisamberg of 120 kW,
a splendid nearly completed broadcasting house and over
620,000 licences. The annexation of the Sudeten regions and
the occupation of Czechoslovakia spelt the end of the semi-
official society *Radiojournal* founded in 1923. With its 1,130,000
subscribers it was one of the best of the European broadcast
services ; it owned eight stations, among them Prague I
of 120 kW, Melnik of 60 kW and the 34 kW short-wave centre
at Podiebrad, and some thirty studios. Today some of these
stations work unter the same regime as the German transmitters, with the only difference that the technical operation
is controlled by the Protector of Bohemia and Moravia. Three
stations, Prague I, Brno, and Moravska-Ostrava, are managed
by a new organization, the *Cesky Rozhlas*, which is responsible
for the programmes for the Czech population. The licences
in the Protectorate numbered 930,134 on January 1, 1942.

---

[1] Stations in the occupied countries and territories are also
considered as "German stations". *Cf. Rundfunkarchiv*, Oct. 1941.

[2] *Rundfunkarchiv*, 1941, May, pp. 193-94 ; July, pp. 290-96,
October, pp. 433-34 ; December, pp. 524-27 ; March 1942, pp. 135-
37.

[3] The development and organization of the radio in these
countries is described in detail in our book *La Radiodiffusion,
Puissance Mondiale*, Paris 1937.

In Slovakia too there was founded a new society called *Slovensky Rozhlas* which, with the help of three stations, carries on a fairly important activity. The number of receivers, very small as yet, was 91,835 on January 1, 1942. It should also be noted that the station of Kosice was ceded to Hungary together with that region [1].

With Poland was also dismembered the important network of the national society *Polskie Radjo*, which at the end of July 1940 served over one million subscribers and was formed of ten stations, including the 120 kW long-wave transmitter Warsaw I, and four 50 kW regional stations. The majority of them fell in 1939 to Germany, three (Baranowicze, Luck and Lwow) to the Soviet Union and one (Vilna) to Lithuania. Since the occupation of the territory by the armies of the Reich, all Polish stations are run by the RRG and the German postal authorities. It is the same with the Baltic stations— operated formerly by the official services of Estonia, Latvia and Lithuania—and the stations of the occupied territories in Russia, most of which however appear to have been destroyed. Twelve Baltic, Polish and Russian transmitters, including those of Riga, Kaunas, Reval, Vilna, Baranowicze and Minsk, now form the new German service called *Sendergruppe Ostland;* three Soviet stations form the *Sendergruppe Ukraine*, headed by the station of Kiev.

In Denmark and in Norway the occupying authorities have allowed the broadcasting organizations to remain ; these had for a long time been state controlled. But the change of personnel has also changed the policy of programmes formerly noted for their liberal spirit. The State Broadcasting of Denmark—*Statsradiofonien*—created already in 1926 and from all points of view exemplary, was the tribune of the whole nation; in the "Radiorradet", especially responsible for the programmes, there were—besides three government delegates—four representatives for the principal political parties, two for the press and six for the big listeners' associations. A special commission and thirteen advisory committees assisted the programmes service, whose directors enjoyed

---

[1] Jugoslavia and Greece, see under "Balkan Countries", p. 83.

wide freedom of action. The revenue from the annual licences of ten crowns, wholly devoted to the needs of the radio service, provided for the running of the three stations—Kalundborg, (60 kW), Copenhagen, (10 kW) and the short-wave transmitter at Skamlebaek (6 kW)—as well as the transmissions of an experimental FM transmitter. Broadcasting is very popular in Denmark : in January 1942 there were 900,000 licences ; with 234 sets per thousand inhabitants, almost all homesteads had receivers. The Norwegian service *Norsk Rikskringkasting* was reorganized and transformed from a public utility society into a government department ; the Board of Directors and the Advisory Council gave place to a Director-General, the plenipotentiary of the new government. Henceforth the 19 stations, among them the 100 kW transmitter at Stavanger and the 60 kW long-wave station at Oslo [1], are operated in accordance with the ruling of the occupying authorities. The progress of broadcasting seems to have been seriously impeded : the increase of receivers was merely 6,000 in 1940 as compared with 59,000 in 1939 and the "density" of sets has even been slightly lowered ; licences numbered 456,288 at the end of March 1941.

A special service is working too in the Netherlands, but it has nothing in common with the former broadcasting organizations. Yet the latter largely answered the interests and the needs of the listeners who in fact themselves managed the stations through their various associations whether general, denominational or political, and to whom they paid millions of florins. It had thus been possible to develop a unique radio regime which during fifteen years had been well tested ; private initiative, encouraged by the government, had ensured the working of stations as important as the long-wave transmitter at Kootwijk (120 kW), the transmitters of Hilversum (60 kW) and Jaarsveld (17 kW), and two 60 kW short-wave transmitters at Huizen, belonging to the Philips Company and working specifically for the Dutch East Indies. The programmes, also relayed by numerous wire broadcast services, were extremely varied and enjoyed great popularity.

---

[1] The station of Vigra, of 100 kW, has had to reduce its power to 1 kW, *cf. Norsk Programblad*, August 1941.

At the end of 1940 all the stations and the 800 relay-exchanges
were placed under the sole control of the state which keeps to
itself the right of broadcasting programmes [1]. Consequently,
the radio associations were dissolved and replaced by an
official service *Rijksradio Omroep de Nederlandsche Omroep*
affiliated to the Ministry of Education and Arts ; the property
of the associations, particularly the studios at Hilversum,
was taken over by the state service. At the same time a licence
fee (of 9 florins per annum) was imposed upon listeners ; all
infringement of ordinances concerning the declaration of
receivers and the payment of taxes is to be punished, the
penalties being up to six months imprisonment or fines up to
the amount of 1,000 florins [2]. The long-wave station, called
henceforth "Grossender Friesland", is used exclusively for
German broadcasts. The transmitters of Hilversum and
Jaarsveld have been replaced by a single station situated at
Lopik and having two transmitters, of 125 kW each [3]. As
the present Director-General has stressed, programmes must
now reflect the "new political and cultural orientation".
Here too the development of the radio has been seriously
affected ; the number of listeners and subscribers to the
relay exchanges had in the spring of 1941 fallen from 1,440,626
to 1,135,379, and this loss has not yet entirely been made
good.

Belgium also had an excellent service, managed since 1930
by the *Institut National Belge de Radiodiffusion* (INR). The
radio activity took into account the requirements of Walloons
and Flemings, as well as of the political and religious tendencies,
reflected in the composition of the board of management and
in the active cooperation in the programmes of eight listeners'
associations. The two official 15 kW stations at Brussels-Velthem
broadcast one in French, the other in Flemish ; sixteen small
private stations promoted the commercial interests of the
country through their local advertising programmes, meanwhile a government short-wave station ensured the link with
the Belgian Congo. When the German troops entered Brussels,

[1] Ordinances of the Reich Commissioner, dated December 19,
1940 and March 12, 1941.

[2] *Cf. Bulletin IBU*, May 1941, p. 143.

[3] *Ibidem*, August 1941, p. 246.

the broadcasting house, the most modern in Europe and completed shortly before the war, was empty ; its technical equipment had been taken away or destroyed [1], as was also the case with the Velthem station. The occupying authorities had therefore to rebuild transmitters, managed today on the model of the German stations and directed by an Administrator appointed by the military Commander. Broadcasts in French and in Flemish are transmitted by three medium-wave stations ; all private services have been suppressed. The audience has not increased latterly, on the contrary, the number of receivers has fallen during 1940 from 1,148,659 to 1,102,130 and no new data are available.

The service of the Grand-Duchy of Luxemburg has been entirely abolished. The *Compagnie Luxembourgeoise de Radiodiffusion*, the chief private and commercial company in Europe, created in 1930 largely with foreign capital, has been dissolved and its 200 kW station attached to the German network.

The stations in Occupied France have suffered the same fate ; since the armistice, they are controlled and administered by the German authorities. Among them are the best and most powerful of the country, especially "Radio-Paris" which had a new technical equipment of 450 kW, Rennes-Bretagne (120 kW), Bordeaux-Lafayette (60 kW) and the new 100 kW short-wave centre "Paris-Mondial" [2]. With the exception of certains hours when certain transmitters are "lent" to the French Government the stations of the occupied zone broadcast programmes provided by the German society. The listeners, meanwhile, seem as yet to be linked with the French broadcasting authorities ; at least the licences are listed in the statistics of the French broadcasting service.

It is hardly necessary to insist on the fact that the German radio regulations concerning the reception of foreign stations

---

[1] Franz Köppe "Der Belgische Rundfunk", *Rundfunkarchiv*, Berlin, January 1941.

[2] Four stations, Paris PTT, Lille, Strasbourg, and Dijon have been put out of action owing to military operations. *Cf.* the article of Commandant Duvivier, director general of the French state service, in *Radio National*, October 19, 1941.

are valid too in all these territories and that the occupying authorities severely penalize those who disobey the law [1].

France

The French radio has changed with the political situation : the democratic regime has been succeeded by a totalitarian one ; the liberal and individualist attitude which was so long characteristic of French broadcasting and which permitted the co-existence of a state service and a dozen private societies, is no longer allowed. The new organization is ruled by the same authoritarian principle as that applied to the German radio and one of the first acts of the government was to suppress the numerous advisory committees, especially the boards of management ("Conseils de Gérance") which collaborated in the artistic activity of the regional stations. Now, the French state service, called *Radiodiffusion Nationale Française*, placed under the Vice-President of the Council and the secretary general of information, is directed by a Director-General and the heads of the different sections [2]. The main source of revenue is still the licence fee, 90 francs for the private use of a receiver, 180 or 360 francs for receivers used in public buildings. To this is added a tax on valves and the revenue from an official review, which replaces the fifteen pre-war radio magazines.

The private stations, grouped in the *Fédération Française de Radiodiffusion* are also now under state control. Similarly, the national broadcasting service exercises its authority over the stations of Algeria, the colonies, the protectorates, mandated countries and territories.

The armistice obliged France immediately to suppress all broadcasting activities. Only later, on the basis of agreements concluded with the German authorities, was the government at Vichy able gradually to resume work on certain medium-wave stations in the non-occupied zone and since August 11,

---

[1] For listening to and relating news of the "enemy" Norwegians were recently condemned to death. *Cf. Rundfunkarchiv*, March 1942, p. 123.

[2] Law of October 1, 1941. *Cf. Bulletin IBU*, January 1942, pp. 2-3.

1941 also on short waves, but under German control.
Working conditions are extremely difficult, owing first to the
division of the country into two zones. Moreover it has not
been possible to centralize all the services in the same town ;
the general directorate is at Vichy, with the government,
which gives out the news and the current events broadcasts ;
the artistic services are at Marseilles and the technical and
administrative services at Toulouse [1].

Of the sixteen government stations and the twelve private
stations only a small number, and not the best, are still at
the disposal of the French radio. It has consequently been
necessary to substitute for the numerous national and regional
transmissions of the official stations a single programme
broadcast by one chain of seven stations during the day, and
six at night. As for the six private stations situated in the free
zone and also forming a chain, they broadcast, besides official
information, entertainment programmes during a few hours.

Limited technical means and present difficulties notwithstanding, the French broadcasters endeavour to reconstruct the
radio service. Their tasks are numerous : political propaganda,
collaboration with the social work institutions and, above all,
the fight against depression. By means of the new 100 kW
short-wave station at Allouis, the national service also broadcasts, from Vichy, daily programmes intended for the French
Empire and entitled "La Voix de la France".

Formerly the international element was very important
in the French programmes and there were even private stations
which broadcast English publicity for hours. Today the
listening in to British stations and to all stations opposed to
the political views of the government of Vichy is forbidden [2].

In January 1942, the number of French licences totalled
5,263,000, i.e. a density of 125.60°/oo. But only one quarter
of the listeners reside in the non-occupied zone.

---

[1] Cf. Bulletin IBU, December 1940, pp. 332-34.
[2] As penalties the law provides for internment in a concentration
camp, closing of public buildings, fines up to 10,000 francs or
three years' imprisonment. Cf. Der Rundfunkhändler, Berlin
November 19, 1941.

Italy

The Italian radio has many features similar to the German. A political instrument like the press and the cinema, it has ever acted as the interpreter of the Fascist party. Although the monopoly is granted (until 1952) to a private society—the *Ente Italiano per le Audizioni Radiofoniche (EIAR)*—the radio is run on the lines of a government service. Through the medium of the Minister of Popular Culture and a supervisory committee, the state exercises direct influence on the management of stations and the composition of programmes. For the broadcasting of all political matter, the Italian stations must have special permission, and no one can speak over the microphone without the consent of the government.

Internal organization is provided for by the General Directorate in Rome and sub-directorates at each of the main stations. The necessary funds come from all kinds of sources : annual licence fees of 81 lire for private sets and of 150 to 600 lire for receivers in publics places ; taxes on the price of receivers sold ; revenue from the official programme magazine and limited advertising, allowed only in the form of artistic broadcasts.

The Italian network, made up of 40 stations, was until 1940 divided into three chains, broadcasting three alternative programmes ; the key-stations were Rome I of 100 kW, Turin I and Milano I of 30 and 50 kW, and for the third chain Naples I of 10 kW. Of the 9 short-wave transmitters of the "Centro Imperiale" at Rome-Prato Smeraldo some are using 25 and 50 kW, the others 100 kW. (There is another short-wave station in the Vatican City, but it is entirely independent of the Italian network [1].)

Moreover the EIAR operates a powerful station in Lybia, that of Tripoli (50 kW), and several small transmitters in Albania and the Jugoslav territories which are under Italian domination [2].

---

[1] See part B. IV, p. 137.
[2] Until 1940 it also ran the station at Addis Abeba. See B III, p. 121.

The number of alternative programmes has had to be diminished, and since Italy's entry into the war, listeners are obliged to rest content with one main programme, to which is added during part of the day a secondary programme and "propaganda broadcasts". Musical and dramatic broadcasts have been reduced in favour of the information service and of "documentary" programmes. Special attention is paid to broadcasts for soldiers, to the transmission of news from home and from the front, and to programmes for the wounded, for workers, for peasants, for schools and for the youth organizations. The school and agricultural broadcasts are done in close connection with an educational and political institution, the *Ente Radio Rurale*, which is in charge of these programmes and of the organization of listening in the schools and small villages, to which it distributes thousands of receivers.

To political activity within the country is added extensive international propaganda [1]. Anxious to interest foreign listeners in Fascist ideas and in Italian language and culture, the EIAR has since 1934 spoken to them ; it has even founded a "Radio-University" which gives courses in eight languages.

The number of receivers was for a long time very limited, barely half a million in 1936. That is why, with the support of the government, the EIAR launched a big campaign on behalf of the radio, with the result that in January 1942 the number of licences was 1,675,000 ; as yet however there are only 36.9 receivers per thousand inhabitants. But one must not lose sight of the fact that collective listening is widely prevalent, especially in the country districts, and that the rebroadcasting of programmes in Lybia and in certain regions in the Balkans considerably increases the size of the audience which hears the Italian transmissions.

Balkan Countries

The conditions of broadcasting in the Balkan countries were never very favourable. The propagation of waves is difficult in these mountainous regions and the stations, working more or

---

[1] In Italy too, it is forbidden to listen to "enemy and neutral" broadcasts and the penalties inflicted on offenders were trebled in 1941, reaching 30,000 lire.

less singly, hardly succeed in "covering" the national territories. The limited financial means do not permit of any great extension of the service ; finally the numbers and the density of receivers are among the lowest in Europe. It is only around 1937 that, in most of these countries, radio conditions began to improve.

This progress has been seriously affected by the war, which has interfered with the beginnings of improvement. Broadcasting in Jugoslavia clearly shows the extent of the upheaval. Of the three private stations in Ljubljana, Zagreb and Belgrade, the first is today run by the Italian authorities, the second by the new Croat state service, and the third—like the official short-wave station of Belgrade—by a German "Propaganda-Kompanie"[1]. Not one of them can meet the needs of its particular region and that is why new transmitters must be established. The revenue from the licences—which numbered 177,405 at the end of 1940—will in future be divided between three countries and doubtless much money will have to be invested in the radio before it can begin to show a profit. Two new societies have been created in Serbia : *Radio-Belgrad A. G.* and *Teleradio A. G.*, one of which will operate the standard broadcast stations, and the other the short-wave transmitters[2].

Yet other stations work under the control of the Axis, such as the little transmitters of Albania, and the two stations of Greece, which, for long hostile to broadcasting, had created a national service only in 1938. The Athens station of 15 kW has since October 26, 1941 been run by a new society, the *Griechische Rundfunk A.G.* (AERE), founded with German help and a capital of 500,000 Reichsmarks[3]. The number of Greek listeners, though doubled in 1939, still remains small ; in January 1940 it was 54.600 or 8.79 °/oo.

In Rumania, broadcasting has followed the political development. In January 1941, the service was militarized ; shortly afterwards the Board of Directors was dissolved, its powers being transferred to an officer who is simultaneously director general and military commissioner[4]. It appears, however,

[1] *Cf. Weltrundfunk*, Nov./Dec. 1941, p. 23.
[2] *Cf. Der Rundfunkhändler*, Berlin, September 24, 1941.
[3] *Cf. Rundfunkarchiv*, October 1941.
[4] *Cf. Ibid.*, May 1941, p. 182.

that the radio society retains its semi-official character and that
two-fifths of the capital remain in private hands. But it has
had to give up its monopoly and countenance the formation
in Bucharest of a society *Interradio A.G.* created with
German financial assistance and having as its aim the building
and operating of stations in the Balkans and the Near-East.
Present difficulties are serious. Three stations must cover
the whole country : "Radio-Romania" at Brasov (long waves)
of 150 kW, Bucharest of 12 kW and "Radio-Moldova" at
Jassy inaugurated on November 2, 1941 and replacing "Radio-
Bessarabia" destroyed by the Russian troops during their
retreat [1]. As the network has to be reconditioned the government has decreed (on September 29, 1941) a considerable
increase in the licence fees, carried from 360 to 900 Lei for
detector sets, from 780 to 1680 lei for valve receivers when
in private use, and up to 9000 lei in public buildings and
business firms [2]. The somewhat limited number of receivers
has further diminished in 1940 from 316,664 to 244,309. Until
January 1942, and in spite of the re-occupation of Bessarabia,
this loss had not been entirely made good ; there were only
284,000 licences and a density of 16.70 $^o/_{oo}$.

After the formation in 1935 of an official service and the
setting up of a 100 kW national transmitter at Sofia, Bulgaria
could hope that its radio service might have a rapid development. But that hope has not been fulfilled, during the past
year however some progress has been made thanks to the
annexation of the former Serbian transmitter of Skoplje (20
kW) and to the increase in licences from 83,000 to 156,000.
Even now the density is only 17.61 $^o/_{oo}$.

The radio situation is more favourable in Turkey which,
having so far been spared warfare, was able better to develop
its service ; its strategic position between Europe and Asia

---

[1] *Ibidem*, November 1941, p. 373. The Russian transmitters
of Odessa and Tiraspol were recently incorporated into the
Rumanian service.

[2] It should be noted that the licence system in Rumania, the
most complicated in the world, has different tariffs for each
category of receivers and subscribers, further distinguishing
between the usage and the placing of receivers. *Cf.* our study
"Les droits d'écoute dans le monde", *Journal des Télécommunications*
September 1939.

gives it today a special importance. After years of trials and unsuccessful efforts broadcasting became state controlled in 1936. The new organization *Radio-Ankara* was given a powerful station composed of three transmitters, one operating with 60 kW and 120 kW on long waves, the two others with 20 kW on short waves. The very high licence fees and taxes on imported receivers together with the revenue from limited publicity maintain the service. Besides programmes in the national language, numerous broadcasts are given in English, French, and the languages of the Balkan peoples and of the Near East. The audience is steadily increasing : at the beginning of 1942 there were in Turkey (European and Asiatic) 101,983 licences, double the number that is of 1939 ; the "density" of receivers, however, is as yet small : 5.71 per thousand inhabitants.

Hungary

Based on a long standing tradition and developed through the common efforts of the state and a private society, broadcasting in Hungary has a privileged position and one which the war does not seem to have shaken.

Fifty years ago, Budapest enjoyed the novelty of regular transmission of news and music ; a collaborator of Edison's had set up a wire distribution service, working under the name of "Telefon Hirmondó" (Telephone Journal), and when in 1925 radio broadcasting was introduced in the country, the government granted the concession to the same company. Called henceforth *Magyar Telefon Hirmondó és Rádió* it runs the artistic and intellectual work in cooperation with the Administration of Posts and Telegraphs which owns all the technical equipment.

The state, represented on the Board of Directors, controls the programmes through a government commission, on which sit representatives of various ministries.

The main source of revenue comes from licence fees to which are added the subscriptions to the wire broadcast service. Receipts are equally divided between the radio and the state ; after the 400,000th licence, however, only 20% goes to the society.

The Hungarian network is formed of seven standard broadcast transmitters ; the key-station, of 120 kW, is at Budapest, where there also operates a 20 kW station [1], and a 5 kW short-wave station. Radio broadcasting and wire broadcasting form one service and complement each other. The majority of listeners use direct reception ; the "Telephone Journal" numbers several thousand subscribers in the capital and also serves about 16,000 hospital beds, provided with earphones. The number of licences increases steadily, and rose from 610,000 in January, 1941 to 750,000 at the beginning of 1942.

U.S.S.R.

The broadcasting system of the U.S.S.R. is related to that of other totalitarian countries. The conception is the same, the radio being a government service and the voice of the ruling party. The differences lie only in the special tasks of the Soviet radio, tasks which are due to the extent of the territory, the great diversity of peoples in the Union—numbering two-hundred —and lastly the poverty of a large part of the population. These factors have influenced the radio organization and led the authorities to add to the activity of the central service that of numerous regional services and to develop, on a scale hitherto unknown, the habit of collective listening or rather the listening of collectivities.

The supreme authority in broadcasting matters is the People's Commissariat of Communications (Narkomsviaz), owner of the technical equipment of the stations and of most of the relay exchanges. But the management itself is in the hands of the *Committee for Radiofication and Radio Broadcasting connected with the Council of People's Commissars*, created in 1933 and endowed with very wide powers. It is in charge of the organization and the direction of the radio service ; its complex activities range from laboratory work to the building of stations, from the transmission of programmes to the reception of

---

[1] Provisionally not in operation.

them. To this technical and political mission is added also an educational mission. For the radio must give the people, left ignorant during centuries, the rudiments of knowledge and develop their intellectual capacities.

Internal organization reflects the authoritarian principle : the programmes are arranged, without the assistance of any advisory commission, according to the instructions of an administrative committee appointed by the Council of People's Commissars.

The finances depend on the general and local budgets of the various states in the Union. The revenue is derived from the licence fees, which draw a distinction between the individual and the collective use of receivers ; from subscriptions to wire broadcasting services ; from public performances and concerts organized by the Radio Committee ; from the transmission of announcements of public interest (a form of limited publicity) ; from subscriptions to educational courses, and finally from the subsidies granted to local radio institutions by various economic and social organizations.

In order to ensure the distribution of programmes throughout the vast territory, the Radio-Committee has set up 90 stations, the principal one, Moscow-Komintern, with a power of 500 kW and six with 100 kW. Long distance broadcasts for Asiatic regions and foreign countries are also done by four big short-wave stations, of which Moscow RW96 has 100 kW. At the beginning of the war, the Soviet network had been considerably enlarged towards the north, the west, and the south by the annexing of the eight stations of the Baltic states incorporated in the U.S.S.R., three powerful Polish stations, two Finnish and one Rumanian transmitters. All these stations have been lost thanks to the course of war, together with twelve Russian stations.

An essential feature of the Soviet radio system are the thousands of relay exchanges [1] which distribute by wire the programmes of the central stations and themselves organize a few hours of programmes of a regional and local nature. Set up in the towns and villages, they are connected especially

---

[1] There were 7,000 in the summer of 1936.

with the political and workers' organizations, the factories and collective farms.

In their broad outlines, the programmes are dominated by political propaganda and education which are closely linked together. Years ago one quarter of the local programmes, over 25,000 hours, was already reserved for propaganda broadcasts ; but the "self-education" programmes are no less important, and serve to supplement the teaching of the universities, schools and correspondence courses.

The major part of the local programmes are broadcast in the languages of the various regions ; in Transcaucasia for instance Georgian, Armenian and Turkish is used as well as Russian. The Soviet stations used to broadcast, already before the war, in 62 different languages and dialects.

Listening is controlled in the sense that the majority of listeners receive the programmes selected by the official relay exchanges and that a good number of individual receivers can only get the local stations. But listeners and especially radio amateurs [1] have always been considered as the best collaborators of the broadcasting service. They are asked to assist in the technical development and, according to their special knowledge, in the building of programmes ; often, the listeners have proved to be the authors of very interesting programmes, especially in the domains of music and the radio drama.

The number of listeners is difficult to indicate precisely. Even the official sources are contradictory, based sometimes on the number of receivers and subscriptions to the relay exchanges, at other times on estimates of the numbers of listeners. We must limit ourselves to noting the rise as indicated by the official figures for Russia in Europe. These give 3,602,800 licences at the beginning of 1936—2,989,800 subscribers to the wire broadcasting services and 613,000 owners of receivers—and 10,551,361 licences at the end of September 1940, of which 4,441,000 receivers. In the same period the density rose from 22.12 to 62.07 $^o/_{oo}$ and it is clear that collective listening greatly increases the radio audience.

---

[1] There are 500,000 young amateurs in the U.S.S.R. see *Bulletin IBU*, June 1941, p. 194.

Scandinavian Countries

Nowhere in Europe has the development of the radio been as successful as in Scandinavia. Each of the countries was able to create an important service whose activities were welcomed by populations genuinely interested in all intellectual and cultural questions. Moreover fruitful collaboration between broadcasters had enriched the programmes of numerous relays and allowed common broadcasts to flourish. But the Russo-Finnish war and especially the occupation of Denmark and Norway [1] have seriously hindered the development of Scandinavian broadcasting. There is only one country where rapid progress continues—Sweden which today ranks among the first of the radio countries.

This progress is due largely to the enterprise of the private limited company *Aktiebolaget Radiotjänst,* responsible for the programme service ; one-third of its shares belongs to the radio industry, two-thirds to the Swedish press. The state deals with the technical operation of the official stations through the Telegraph Administration and leaves the society a fairly wide autonomy, limiting itself to controlling the programmes transmitted. Advisory committees help in the composition of special programmes, particularly the religious broadcasts, the medical, technical or agricultural lectures. Finally numerous radio clubs, owning small broadcasting stations, work in close collaboration with "Radiotjänst".

The broadcasting service is financed by an annual licence fee of ten crowns, from which benefit not only the state and the radio society, but also the private broadcasters, who receive up to 15,000 crowns in subsidies and are able to relay free of charge the programmes of "Radiotjänst". Their fourteen transmitters, which serve as relay stations, complete the national network and form, together with the seventeen official stations, a long chain throughout the country. The programmes are transmitted from Stockholm, the broadcasting centre with a station of 55 kW, to the various provincial stations, of which the most important, Falun and Horby,

---

[1] See "Germany", p. 76-77.

have 100 and 60 kW respectively. Further, a "national" programme, arranged with the active participation of the regional stations, is sent out by the 150 kW long-wave station of Motala. Finally an official short-wave station with two 12 kW transmitters broadcasts programmes intended for Swedish people abroad, especially the three million resident in the United States.

The programmes, of a remarkably high standard, reflect the preoccupation with neutrality and national defence. All the classes of the population, all political parties and opinions have access to the microphone. Since 1940 the society organizes numerous patriotic programmes whose aim is "to consolidate the unity of the country in wartime, to strengthen the will to defend the liberty and independence of the nation"[1]. The educational work is highly praiseworthy ; it enjoys the assistance of the school authorities and of the famous universities of Uppsala and Lund. In order to increase the effect of its programmes, the radio service cooperates with hundreds of "listening groups".

Since 1933 the audience has grown astonishingly ; with its 1,550,691 licences on January 1, 1942, Sweden comes immediately after the great powers and ranks above them as regards the density of receivers. This is 243.4 $^o/_{oo}$ for the whole country, it reached 296.6 $^o/_{oo}$ in Stockholm and even 317.3 $^o/_{oo}$ at Oxlosund. Soon the whole nation will be listening.

Broadcasting in Finland, on the other hand, suffers today—though to a lesser extent than the occupied Scandinavian countries—from the consequences of political events. Formerly moved by the pacifist spirit and that desire for independence which has always inspired the people, broadcasting has become an instrument of war and propaganda and is today under foreign influence[2]. The organization itself has not changed, the management of the fifteen stations remaining with the society *O.Y. Suomen Yleisradio A.B.*, 90% of whose shares belong to the state. The progress of broadcasting, so regular

---

[1] *Bulletin IBU*, May 1941, p. 164.

[2] Daily the Finnish stations relay many German programmes, especially those intended for the troops of the Reich.

in normal times, appears to be temporarily arrested : the national station of Lahti, one of the most powerful in the world, has been obliged to reduce its power from 220 to 150 kW[1], and the increase of licences has slowed down. On January 1, 1942, there were 374,820 receivers, *i.e.* 120.06 per thousand inhabitants.

The occupation of Iceland by the Anglo-American troops has apparently not affected broadcasting which retains its complete independence. Its activity is a convincing proof of the fact that even in a poor and sparsely populated country, it is possible to develop an extremely valuable service. The organization is modelled on that of Denmark, to whom Iceland was tied through links with the crown. The post office ensures the technical work, a national institution named *Rikisutvarpid* (Iceland State Broadcasting Service) provides the programmes which are controlled by a Council, whose president is appointed by the Minister of Education, while the four members are elected by Parliament. To meet the expenses of a service which is very difficult and costly in this country, the society has recourse to several sources of revenue : licence fee of 30 crowns a year ; radio advertising ; publications ; and finally the sale of receivers and accessories, of which it enjoys the monopoly [2]. The broadcasting centre of Reykjavik has two transmitters, one of 100 kW (long-wave), the other of 7 kW (short-wave) ; a relay station at Eidar helps the distribution of programmes in the eastern side of the island. In its programmes, the official service has always maintained a neutral and liberal attitude, allowing a great many political discussions and electoral debates. The development of Icelandic broadcasting is reflected in the licence figures : the 20,910 receivers declared at the beginning of 1942 represent the very high proportion of 170.69 per thousand inhabitants.

Eire (*Ireland*)

Politically autonomous, the Irish Free State has since 1926 had its own broadcast service, clearly separate from the Northern

---

[1] *Bulletin IBU*, September 1941.

[2] Jonas Thorbergsson, *Broadcast in Iceland*, Reykjavik 1938.

Ireland service, which is affiliated to the BBC. It is also quite differently organized from the services in most British Dominions. The government itself directs the radio, controlled through the Parliament. The management is in the hands of a special department of the Ministry of Posts and Telegraph, *Radio Eireann* which is supported by official subsidies and the revenue from limited advertising. The authorities levy a licence fee and taxes on imported receivers.

There is a 100 kW station at Athlone, assisted by two small transmitters in the principal towns, Cork and Dublin. The programmes and the spoken broadcasts especially, reflect a strong nationalist tendency. Although the English language still predominates, there are hundreds of broadcasts in Gaelic: talks, discussions and news bulletins. School broadcasting is very successful, and even more so is the musical activity which has made the radio service into the chief artistic organization of the country.

The increase of licences is as yet not satisfactory, and the density is far lower than that of Northern Ireland. With 183,300 licences in January 1942, it was 61.8 per thousand.

Iberian Peninsula

The countries of the Iberian Peninsula are, like those of the Balkans, behind in the general development of broadcasting. That is especially true of Spain where political conflicts have seriously affected the radio, which also suffered from the excessive rivalry between the owners of the 66 (!) private stations. A few transmitters excepted, they had no real importance and the broadcasts, filled with commercial announcements, were mostly of little interest. During the civil war, they were divided into two camps. Republicans and Nationalists used them for their propaganda and waged a preliminary ''war on waves''. On coming into power, the nationalist government placed all the stations under official control and established a state service. First the radio was attached to the General Directorate of Propaganda of the Ministry of the Interior. But, following on a recent reorganization, the technical service and the programmes service are separated, the one being henceforth dependent on the Telecommunications

Service, the other on the under-secretariat of the Spanish phalange for popular culture [1]. Some twenty standard broadcast stations and two short-wave stations are operated by *Radio Nacional de España*, financed by licence fees. There are besides dozens of small private stations—about fifty and according to some even sixty—which are obliged to broadcast the national programmes, but allowed to add local and advertising broadcasts of an artistic character. The authorities are endeavouring to reduce the number of stations, to replace them by better equipped and more powerful stations and improve the quality of the programmes.

But in spite of official efforts, the situation is far from satisfactory. Spain lacks powerful stations—the strongest being only of 20 to 30 kW and those of Madrid and Barcelona even of 3 and 5 kW ; the number of licences, estimated at 350,000 at the beginning of 1940, had fallen to 288,000 in January 1942, that is from 15.9 to 11.15 per thousand inhabitants. And the high number of clandestine listeners, mentioned in certain official pronouncements [2], indicates that there yet remains much to be done before the reorganization may bear fruit.

Broadcasting in Portugal also meets with serious difficulties which the official service nevertheless hopes to be able soon to overcome. Recently reorganized, the *Emissora Nacional de Radiodifusora* is run by a board of three members, created by the government and presided over by the director of the Secretariat of National Propaganda.

The official service is charged with the operation of the national transmitters, with the distribution of programmes in the country and the colonies, and with contributing to national propaganda abroad. For these ends it receives the revenue from licence fees, from gifts and subsidies, after deduction of the expenses for the technical service run by the postal administration ; at Lisbon it uses a 20 kW medium-wave and a 5-10 kW short-wave station, and controls several regional and colonial transmitters (the latter belonging to radio-clubs in Angola, Mozambique and Macao).

---

[1] *Bulletin IBU*, July 1941, p. 207.

[2] *Ibid.*, p. 235.

The increase in the number and the proportion of receivers is fairly regular ; on January 1, 1942, these numbered 113,730, *i.e.* 14.76 per thousand inhabitants. There is besides an important 60 kW private station in the small republic of Andorra, operating on medium and short waves ; it broadcasts every evening commercial programmes of an entertaining nature. But in order to avoid all political friction, "Radio-Andorra" refrains from all transmission of information and news.

Switzerland

The Swiss radio has a special place among the European services. Though temporarily attached to a government department, it continues to develop along the same lines and follows the same principles as before the war. Its structure is determined by the special conditions of the country, especially the trilingualism of the population and the very strong regionalist tendencies.

Seven regional societies, grouped since February 1931 within the *Société Suisse de Radiodiffusion (SSR)* [1] are responsible for the elaboration and execution of the three programmes in German, French and Italian ; the technical service, definitely separated from the programme service, is ensured by the General Directorate of Posts and Telegraphs. On the eve of war, the government suspended the concession granted to the SSR and placed the whole service—called henceforth *Service de la Radiodiffusion Suisse (SR)* [2] under the direct control of the Federal Department of Post and Railways [3]. The head of this department gives general instructions on the orientation of programmes, in agreement with the Department for the Interior which is also responsible for the spiritual integrity of the country, for national education and the fine arts. The military authorities, responsible for the control of the news, watch over the radio as they do the press and the cinema. The broadcast service was not however put entirely under

---

[1] "Schweizerische Rundspruch-Gesellschaft" (SRG).
[2] "Schweizerischer Rundspruchdienst" (SR).
[3] Decree of August 29, 1939.

state control. The modifications in the regime do not affect the programmes, arranged as hitherto by the directors and the collaborators of the SSR and the member societies, which have been maintained in their integrity. The licence fee, of 15 francs for ordinary usage, provides the service with the necessary means.

Wire broadcasting is very popular in Switzerland, especially owing to the frequently unsatisfactory conditions for direct reception. On the basis of a concession dated September 25, 1931, the Federal Telephone Administration has developed reception by wire and created relay exchanges which, in the big towns at least, offer their subscribers the three national programmes and a choice of two European programmes. Similarly, two private societies distribute, also by wire, two national programmes and one from abroad.

The composition of programmes is divided between six studios : Basle, Berne and Zürich take turns to provide the programme of the 100 kW national transmitter at Beromünster (and of its relay stations at Basle and Berne) for German-speaking Switzerland ; Geneva and Lausanne do so for the national transmitter at Sottens, operating with the same power (and the relay station at Geneva), for French-speaking Switzerland ; finally, Lugano provides the broadcasts of the 15 kW national transmitter of Monte Ceneri for Italian-speaking Switzerland. A 25 kW short-wave station at Schwarzenburg ensures liaison with the Swiss living abroad and offers programmes in the three national languages and in English. A second short-wave station at Prangins is run on autonomous lines, and was before the war used by the League of Nations [1]. Most of the regional societies own very well equipped studios and buildings which offer all facilities for the broadcasting service.

The special task of the Swiss radio is to develop understanding and feeling for unity between the populations whose languages and cultures differ. Applying the principle of an educational and cultural mission serious efforts have been made during ten years in school broadcasting which has (especially in the German-speaking regions) an important place in the pro-

---

[1] See B.IV "Radio-Nations", pp. 136-37.

grammes. Also today there are special broadcasts, organized by the Army G.H.Q. and aimed at establishing regular contacts between soldiers and civilians.

The increase of listeners using either direct or indirect reception has been very considerable during the past years. On January 1, 1942 Switzerland had a total of 680,300 licences, of which 92,900 for wire reception, i.e. 159.84 per thousand inhabitants.

II. America

What a contrast is broadcasting in America ! There the geographical, economic and political conditions are wholly different and so also is the structure of the radio and the systems of organization. The broadcasters have vast spaces before them and, especially in the United States, have at their disposal huge financial possibilities ; four languages suffice to reach the peoples of the two Americas which form two "blocs" united by links of race, of culture, of interests and political conceptions. Enjoying the stimulus of private initiative, sustained by the enthusiasm of listeners, broadcasting could there develop freely and quickly conquer its place in the national life.

Two-thirds of the world's stations are situated on American soil—900 in the United States, about 100 in Canada and 900 in Latin America which, after years of struggle with the greatest difficulties, is witnessing today the development of tremendous radio activity.

United States of America

Even as on the political plane, hegemony in the domain of radio broadcasting belongs to the United States. It is the entertainment of the whole nation, the source of knowledge and information for the masses, the ideal method of advertising, and it is thus an important educational and economic factor. Moreover it serves as a "free platform" for public opinion which can express itself without hindrance ; it is an instrument of national defence and of Pan-American collaboration.

The structure of broadcasting in this country is a logical consequence of its development : the speedy increase in the number of stations demanded laws and regulations to guarantee their proper working ; the competition of broadcast societies continually called forth a fresh stimulus : radio advertising, used since 1923, gives broadcasters the necessary funds, and the passionate interest of the American people has acted as an encouragement.

The technical service, regulated and controlled by the Federal Government, private ownership and operation, financed by the "sale of time", animated by the spirit of competition and the ardour of a faithful public—such are the fundamentals of the American radio and the conditions which have governed its tremendous extension.

Technical Regime.

Every citizen and every American society able to use wave lengths—recognized as national property and forming part of the public inheritance—in the "public interest, convenience and necessity", may in principle obtain the licence to operate a station. It is granted by the *Federal Communications Commission* (FCC), responsible for assigning to each station its place in the air, distributing the wave lengths, fixing the power and the broadcasting hours for all stations. For this purpose American territory has been divided into five zones and the transmitters classified according to the kind of service they must give : national, regional or local, urban or rural. The wave lengths are allocated according to this plan ; they are attributed exclusively to certain particularly important and powerful stations, or divided between several stations ; so also is divided the broadcasting time, unlimited for some stations, limited to part of the day for the majority [1]. The control of the Commission extends in some measure to the administrative and financial management of the stations and the general character of their programmes. In order that the law be respected, the FCC uses a powerful weapon : the

---

[1] For further details see our study "La Structure de la Radiodiffusion", *Journal des Télécommunications*, Berne, June 1940, p. 154.

non-renewal of the licence, given only for six months. On several occasions already permission has been withdrawn (or refused) to certain broadcasters who, considering their own interests, had neglected the public interest or had not maintained an absolute impartiality. For, according to American law and usage, the stations, once they accept political broadcasts, must grant the same rights and advantages to the authorized representatives of all parties, especially at election times [1]. But these functions apart, the Federal Commission has no power of censorship over broadcast matter and all interference in the programmes service is strictly forbidden to it [2]. Management is free and all government attempts at interference meet with the most violent opposition from the broadcasters [3], who prefer a severe system of "self-regulation" and "self-control". The government itself, and President Roosevelt especially, have stated several times—quite recently when certain restrictive measures became necessary owing to the political situation—that it was intended to safeguard the rights and the independence of broadcasting.

The Broadcasting Services.

Broadcasting is private property and is run on competitive lines. In order to beat the rival, to attract the attention of the public, each advertiser, each broadcaster, each artist and each speaker must ever make a greater effort. The wholly divergent

---

[1] "If any licensee shall permit any person who is a legally qualified candidate for any public office to use a broadcasting station, he shall afford equal opportunities to all other such candidates for that office in the use of such broadcasting station". The Communications Act of 1934, section 315.

[2] "Nothing in this Act shall be understood or construed to give the Commission the power to censorship over the radio communications or signals transmitted by any radio station, and no regulation or condition shall be promulgated or fixed by the Commission which shall interfere with the right of free speech by means of radio communication." The Communications Act of 1934, section 326.

[3] In 1941 the industry was also in sharp conflict with the Federal Commission which tried to limit the influence of the networks and the number of stations dependent on newspaper interests.

character of the owners of stations and of their aims gives the American service a variegated aspect.

The majority of transmitters belong to commercial broadcasting societies. But there are 300 which are owned or controlled by newspapers, thirty-five educational stations, the property of universities or colleges, ten religious stations, controlled by denominational associations or churches, and some stations operated by municipalities or chambers of commerce.

Hundreds of stations are associated with four companies and affiliated to their "national networks" which cross the country from end to end, from New York to San Francisco. These powerful societies reach tens of millions of listeners with their broadcasts and play a tremendous role in the development of American broadcasting.

The most important of them, the *National Broadcasting Company* (NBC)—founded in 1926 and forming part of the Radio Corporation of America (RCA)—grouped 244 stations at the end of 1941, divided into the Red Network and the Blue Network to which are affiliated stations even in Canada, Cuba, Panama and Hawaii [1]. At all times these networks broadcast numerous simultaneous programmes from their key-stations at New York and from other broadcasting centres, especially from Washington, Chicago, San Francisco and Hollywood. In addition, thousands of international broadcasts are sent out by the NBC's powerful short-wave stations. The *Columbia Broadcasting System* (CBS), founded in 1927, incorporates 127 stations, grouped in one chain whose ramifications also reach out to Canada, Hawaii and Porto Rico. Finally the network of the *Mutual Broadcasting System* (MBS), organized in 1934 and made into a national network in 1936, includes nearly 200 stations ; the majority of these however have only a local reach. Beside the big chains there are numerous regional networks and groups which serve more limited interests and are managed independently or in liaison with the national networks. Four years ago there were already about ten of them, made up generally of 3 to 5 stations. Owing

---

[1] In January 1942 the *Blue Network* was established as a separate company.

to their success their number has increased fourfold ; five of them hawe now 15 to 18 transmitters each. The Don Lee Broadcasting System has as many as 31 stations.

Parallel with the centralisation of stations goes the decentralisation of services to meet the needs of an audience so immense, so varied and so complex. Certain stations work exclusively for a certain group of listeners, some addressing only workers or farmers, others Catholics or Jews, others the negro population. In 1941, 298 stations accepted programmes in foreign languages, broadcast especially for immigrants and their descendants. There are Italian networks (25 transmitters), Polish (20), German (15) and Yiddish (15).

A big organization, the National Association of Broadcasters (NAB), groups the owners and operators of about 500 commercial stations and, as associate members, some 30 industrial concerns and other institutions dealing with the radio. Moreover broadcasters of certain categories—stations belonging to the press, independent stations, educational services—form important groups which champion their special interests.

Commercial Organization.

With a few exceptions all the stations are financed by the sale of time which covers the enormous expenditure of 150 million dollars a year. We may recall that in 1941 the "gross time sales" amounted to 237,600,000 dollars and the "net time sales" to 176,280,000 dollars ; in 1940 the revenues were increased by 13,181,948 dollars from various sources, of which 5,851,371 dollars derived from "sale of talent" [1]. But if over 200 stations make a great deal—some 50 of them have receipts of 500,000 to 1,000,000 dollars and even more—there are as many whose expenditure is higher, at least slightly, than their income.

Time on the air, rated according to the length of the broadcast and the hour chosen, the reach and the number of participating stations, is very expensive. The key-stations of the NBC and

---

[1] FCC Report "1940 Combined Income Statement of US Broadcasters", Washington, May 1941.

the CBS, for instance, ask from 1,200 to 1,400 dollars for one hour, and from 480 to 560 dollars for 15 minutes [1]. The price of one hour on the "basic networks" of the CBS or the NBC (each of which touch 26 towns) comes to 9,885 dollars or 10,780 dollars in the evening and the price for 15 minutes is 3,954 or 4,360 dollars [2] ; these prices increase of course with the number of "supplementary" stations and there is the further cost of the programmes, borne by the advertiser. The network company pays the associated stations which carry the same commercial programme ; these on the other hand pay a certain sum to the society for any other non-commercial programme which is provided for them. The minimum time of an advertising broacast on the big networks is generally a quarter of an hour ; several regional networks and individual stations however also sell minutes for a few dollars.

Nevertheless there are stations which abstain from advertising, such as some of the educational and religious stations, which receive subsidies from universities, denominational institutions, big foundations and sometimes gifts and voluntary contributions.

Stations and Studios.

During eight years the number of standard broadcast stations has not ceased to grow : from 591 in 1934 to 891 in January 1942, not including 22 stations under construction. There are further 11 "international broadcasting stations" operating on short waves and 3 others for which a construction permit has been given [3]. To this must be added 62 commercial and 16 experimental Frequency Modulation (FM) broadcasting stations

---

[1] The great "international stations have been more modest ; for instance, the Bound Brook stations ask from $150 to $300 for Spanish broadcasts, $180 for Portuguese broadcasts and $300 for the English programmes. *Cf.* Rate Card of the NBC International Division, which came into effect Sept. 1, 1941.

[2] Certain reductions in price (though never beyond $12\frac{1}{2}\%$) are granted to important clients who week by week use whole networks and sign annual contracts. Similarly the day rates are reduced by as much as 66 % as compared with the evening.

[3] These figures do not include about 600 transmitters of small power and very short waves, used to relay the programmes from one station to another when the telephone circuits are not available.

(36 of which are already in use), 34 experimental and 8 commercial television stations (19 are already working) and some twenty stations intended for Facsimile Service [1].

Among the standard broadcast stations, forty-two use 50 kW, the maximum power granted at present in the United States. A dozen of them however have applied for permission to increase to 500 kW, and two even to 750 kW. As for the short-wave stations, they all work on very high power : the main ones in South Schenectady and Bound Brook have 100 kW and a new station at San Francisco, directed especially towards the East, will have the same energy ; that of Cincinnati (Mason) uses 75 kW and the majority of the others 50 kW.

Many stations, and the most important, are grouped, as is natural for private and commercial running, in the urban centres and the richest and most thickly populated districts. Thus Chicago has 15 standard broadcast and 7 FM stations, of which five of 50 kW ; New York has 14 standard and 10 FM stations, of which four of 50 kW ; Los Angeles 12 and Philadelphia 9 standard broadcast stations, plus 5 FM transmitters each. There are 12 towns with six to eight stations each and 43 towns with 3 to 5 stations.

The majority of the big stations have the most up-to-date technical equipment which is constantly being improved. In the transmission centres numerous studios are fitted out for all needs, grouped, as for example in New York and Hollywood, in luxurious buildings. Some companies have also acquired theatres where are shown in public the programmes which are particularly important and spectacular.

Programmes.

The extent of the activity of the American stations is clearly shown by the fact that, already four years ago, the

---

[1] See Part C. We might further add that there were also (end 1939) 65,000 amateur stations, 6,300 stations belonging to the police, 5,200 naval stations, nearly 2,500 aeronautical stations and more than 1,000 transmitters situated in the vast forest regions, having as their task the transmission of information in case of fire or accidents. *Cf. Rundfunkarchiv*, Sept., 1941 p. 380, and *Statistique générale des radiocommunications*, 1939, Bureau of the International Telecommunication Union 1940.

programmes lasted 62,000 hours [1] in one week. Today that figure is certainly far higher owing to the increased number to stations (nearly 200 have been added during this period) and to the extension of broadcasting schedules by the majority of stations.

The programmes are divided into two categories, the "commercial programmes", paid for by advertisers and taking about one-third of the time, and the "sustaining programmes", financed directly by the broadcasting companies or provided by the State Departments, universities, educational or religious institutions. Three quarters of the commercial broadcasts are elaborated by specialized agencies and recording services [2] which offer complete programmes and also plan full advertising compaigns [3]. The advertisement is often limited to a few introductory phrases merely quoting the name of the "generous" advertiser who offers his listeners the broadcast in the hope that they may become his future clients. The regional stations affiliated to one of the national networks, relay about 50 to 70% of the programmes organized by the latter ; the remaining time is devoted to regional programmes and especially to recorded music [4].

The programmes, which rarely last beyond a quarter of an hour (or half an hour in the evening), are very varied and entertaining. Whether commercial or non-commercial they run through the whole scale of types of programmes : the first group shows a certain preference for light music ; the second tends more towards the artistic, cultural and educational. The best artistic ensembles and the best American and foreign artists perform in them. Very great care is given to the finish and the "presentation". It is noteworthy that dramatic broadcasts have a great vogue : from 1932 to 1939 the time reserved by the NBC for the radio drama was almost doubled, going from 10.8 to 20.1% of the programme time [5].

---

[1] Programme analysis made by the FCC during the week of March 6, 1938.

[2] Cf. Kenneth G. Bartlett "Trends in Radio Programs", in The Annals, January 1941, p. 23.

[3] In 1941, there were in the U.S.A. about 200 transcription, recording, programme producing, script and related services. Cf. Broadcasting Yearbook 1941, pp. 184-190.

[4] Cf. Kenneth G. Bartlett, ibid., p. 18.

[5] Ibidem, p. 17.

Another popular feature is the tremendous news service which covers all national and international activities. To the news bulletins—which have risen over the same period from 2% to 3.8%—are added interviews, running commentaries and big political broadcasts which make the American radio into the "forum of democracy". Each interesting question in the national life is the subject of discussions allowing the people to learn different points of view [1]. One must also recognize that the American radio, in spite of its commercial structure, lends itself willingly to educational work and gives effective help to the educational departments and institutions of all the states. Similarly the stations never refuse to fulfil the obligations of public service but whenever the occasion arises contribute with all their might to the safeguarding of the national interest, to the protection of life and property. And with the same ardour they have put themselves today at the service of national defence [2], organizing thousands of patriotic broadcasts and special programmes in favour of national loans [3]. Hundreds of commercial stations collaborate voluntarily and free of charge with the army services in order to provide entertainment and news for soldiers in their camps.

The development of Pan American broadcasting—though encouraged by the government, the Pan American Union and the Nelson Rockefeller Committee—is also due to the work of private broadcasters who have not hesitated to build at their own cost powerful "international stations" and to spend hundreds of thousands of dollars on special programmes, mostly in foreign languages. A whole group of societies have followed the example of the NBC which inaugurated already ten years ago its broadcasts for Latin America. Among these are the CBS, World Wide Broadcasting Foundation, Crosley Corporation, General Electric Co., and Westinghouse Co. Collaboration between the broad-

[1] The same liberalism is reflected in the religious broadcasts which have an important place in the non-commercial programmes.

[2] Like the other radio electrical services and industries broadcasting is represented by leading personalities and eminent experts on the Defense Communications Board ; similarly the American army has created a "Broadcasting" section directed by the public relations director of the NAB.

[3] "To promote sale of defence bonds", Toscanini conducted in December 1941 two concerts of the NBC Symphony Orchestra.

casters and the exchange of programmes between the countries of the north and the south increases month by month, especially since the formation of the Latin American networks of the NBC and the CBS.

The American broadcaster has long since won the confidence of his audience, one might almost say of the whole people. Broadcasting today is an integral part of life in the United States. After an increase of 11,000,000 sets in 1940 and 13,000,000 in the following year, there were 30,300,000 "radio homes" and 57,400,000 receivers in January 1942, of which 6,750,000 were in the state of New York, 4,740,000 in Pennsylvania, 4,000,000 in Illinois, 3,700,000 in California, 3,560,000 in Ohio and 1.2 to 2.5 million in ten other states ; over a third of the "radio families" own two or three receivers. In addition to this there are nearly 3 million portable sets and 9,300,000 "auto-sets"[1]. One may thus say without exaggeration that broadcasting reaches almost the whole of the population of 132 millions in the United States.

Canada

Though it has a common frontier with the United States, Canada's radio conditions are wholly different. Everything is more difficult in this country : its vast extent, the five time zones, the bi-lingualism of the population greatly complicate the task of the broadcasters, already complicated enough thanks to the competition of the big American companies. For many years it was impossible to overcome these difficulties ; the commercial stations situated in a few urban centres did not serve the country districts, and a large part of the Dominion was within the reach and influence of the neighbouring stations in the United States. The government, unable to replace the numerous private services by one state service—that would require vast sums—decided on a compromise between the

---

[1] Estimates by Dr. O. H. Caldwell ; cf. *Broadcasting*, January 12 and February 2, 1942. By order of the War Production Board (March 7, 1942), the manufacture of all civilian receiving sets must be suspended on April 22, 1942, in preparation for the full conversion to wartime production of all radio plants. But it is estimated that 3 million sets will have already been produced before the conversion order goes into effect ; this number of receivers plus the sets on retailers' shelves would suffice for the country's needs.

American and the European systems. An official broadcasting Commission was appointed in 1932 to establish a national programme and operate the several low-power stations which the government had acquired. As its activity, though valuable, was not wholly adequate, the authorities following the example of the BBC, founded in 1936 a big public utility company : the *Canadian Broadcasting Corporation* (CBC). Having the status of a public body and controlled by a Council of nine governors, it is independent and responsible only to Parliament. Besides the organization of a national service and the management of the official transmitters, it also controls the activities of all the Canadian stations ; its main aim however is the broadcasting of a programme of high value, capable of contributing to the improvement of the relationship between Canadians who speak English and those who speak French, and to establish cordial and generous relationships between the two chief peoples of the country [1].

The revenue from licences could not suffice for the fulfilment of this task ; the Corporation was therefore allowed to increase the fee by 25% (to 2.5 dollars) and to broadcast advertising programmes to the extent necessary to balance the budget [2]. Since then, the financial situation has greatly improved : in 1934/35 the Commission received only $1,396,000 ; in 1940/41 the Corporation collected $4,092,794, of which $3,140,259 derived from licences and nearly $900,000 from commercial broadcasting ; it was thus able to devote to programmes a sum four times greater than that spent by the Commission, $ 1,721,755 [3].

This improvement is due also to the technical progress achieved by the CBC, which at the present time operates ten of the 87 standard broadcast stations—among them four of 50 kW—and two of the 8 short-wave stations used less for international broadcasts than for long-distance national broadcasts.

The Corporation has inaugurated a happy cooperation with

[1] Canadian Broadcasting Act of June 23, 1936.

[2] Anxious to keep the equilibrium between commercial and non-commercial broadcasts, the CBC refused in 1939/40 commercial contracts of about 250,000 dollars in value.

[3] Official Report for the financial year 1940/41.

the commercial societies and signed in October 1937 a contract providing for the transmission of the official programmes throughout the country. With the help of private stations, it was able to form a national network of 35 stations reaching from one end to the other of the Dominion and made up of 8 regional networks, working for the various provinces. Moreover 36 other private stations carry the non-commercial broadcasts of the CBC, especially official news bulletins which are put at their disposal. To meet the growing demands of advertisers for network evening time [1] the CBC formed (in the summer of 1941) a second network, comprising 23 stations and exclusively reserved for advertising broadcasts ; it will be operated only as and when required by commercial sponsors and only after 6 p.m [2].

The majority of private stations are run by the broadcasting companies, 27 by newspaper firms and two by universities. But the strongest of them only have 10 and 15 kW ; for until now the Corporation has reserved to itself a monopoly of high-powered stations, a monopoly which will probably soon be abolished since the Canadian military authorities are interested in the operation of a great number of powerful stations.

The difference in time, the enormous distances which separate the points whence programmes originate and the profound regional divergencies have necessitated the division of the territory into five main zones, each having a broadcasting centre : Halifax, Montreal, Toronto, Winnipeg and Vancouver. It is in these regions that are organized for preference the official broadcasts which call on local talent. Their number and duration constantly increase ; in 1939/40 the CBC sent out 29,889 programmes (that is 11,000 more than in the preceding year) of a total length of 10,473 hours [3].

The programmes of the Corporation reveal the wish to strengthen national feeling, to favour the creative powers of

---

[1] Canadian broadcasting stations are at present doing more business than ever before, and numerous stations are completely "sold out". *Cf. Broadcasting*, November 1941.

[2] *Cf. Broadcasting*, July 28, 1941, p. 24. — The private broadcasters had hoped to be allowed to make such a network themselves, but the CBC was opposed to the establishing of a second chain giving a complete service.

[3] *Cf.* Annual report of the CBC.

the various regions and foster unity between the provinces. This does not prevent it from relaying on its network the very best programmes that it can get, programmes of the Canadian commercial companies, of the American networks and of the BBC, a substantial part of whose Empire Service is broadcast through the Dominion. The private stations, often under the direct or indirect influence of the societies in the United States, may freely choose their programmes, but are obliged to observe strict rules where political broadcasts and medical publicity is concerned.

Great efforts are devoted to education, especially to school broadcasting and to programmes for farmers which include special bulletins intended for remote regions where newspapers arrive days and in some cases weeks late. The spirit of public service is expressed in a successful activity inaugurated eight years ago : the "Northern Message Service" which every winter transmits free of charge private messages to officers and workers in the arctic regions, since there is no other way of reaching them.

At first the Corporation met with serious opposition within the country—375,000 licences were lost in 1937 ! But since 1939 progress has been assured ; on January 1, 1941 the number of radio homes, having taken a long time to pass the million mark, was 1,676,530, [1] a figure which corresponds to the very high proportion of 148.15 receivers per thousand inhabitants. And the efforts continue in order that the time lost during several years may be regained and Canada move into the front rank of the radio nations.

Newfoundland

There is great interest in the radio in Newfoundland, a country famous in the history of wireless telegraphy ; for it was there that Marconi received in 1901 the first signals that crossed the Atlantic. For a long time half a dozen small stations, all situated at Saint-Johns were responsible for the service and made ends meet as well as they could, some through radio-advertising, others through public subscriptions given for the

---

[1] Figure indicated by the Coverage Statistics Department, CBC.

broadcasting of religious programmes. Today the situation has wholly changed thanks to the creation of an official society : the *Broadcasting Corporation of Newfoundland.* It is organized on the same principle as the Canadian, with which it keeps up very friendly relations and whose non-commercial programmes it relays. The national service owns a new government station of 12,5 kW and is financed by the licence fees, sale of time and the broadcast licences of four private stations which are allowed to continue their activity. Taking recent progress into account it is probable that the continued increase of licences (which reached 11,600 at the beginning of 1940) will maintain its rapid rise.

Latin America

Broadcasting in Latin America, though favoured by the fact that most nations have the same language, has grown slowly and with difficulty and is as yet today far below the level attained in Europe or in North America.

There are compelling reasons for this slowness. In the tropical zones, transmission and reception are seriously affected for months on end by the difficulties of the propagation of waves and serious atmospheric disturbances, by the excessive heat and damp which wear out radio electrical material. On the economic side the obstacles are no fewer : the low standard of living in many countries, the small revenue and consequently the small purchasing power of the majority of inhabitants, the uncertainty of business which depends more or less on the export of one or two national products. Yet other factors have also retarded the development of the radio : confusion in the management due to the multitude of rival societies ; the lack of financial means, hindering the rapid extension of the services ; the defects of a technical order limiting the quality of the transmission and its reach ; and finally the mediocre quality of the programmes, too commercial in spirit and "stuffed" with advertisements.

Thanks however to recent economic progress, to better national and international organization of the service, to technical improvements and the definite betterment of the programmes, it has been possible to overcome, or at least to reduce, the serious difficulties of the beginning. At last today broadcasting in Latin America also begins to fulfil its mission as a political, social, cultural and above all educational instrument.

Since there is affinity between the various Latin American services, we may limit ourselves to setting out their characteristic features. The radio regime is almost everywhere similar to that of the United States of America. There is the same independence in the management which is most often in the hands of individuals and private broadcasting societies. State action, though recently strengthened, is generally limited to supervising the commercial stations and the amateur stations. The few restrictions, not always obeyed, tend above all to minimize the technical shortcomings and prevent excesses of publicity as well as broadcasts inacceptable from the political or moral points of view.

There is however an important difference as compared with the "American system" : a certain number of stations, sometimes the most powerful in the country, are owned and operated by state services.

Expenses are covered by the most varied means. The usual method of financing, the licence fee, does not yield satisfactory results. That "duty", introduced into several countries of Central America and the British Colonies, is very unpopular and listeners use every expedient to avoid it. The state is therefore obliged to write down in the budget the sums necessary for the operation of its stations or broadcast commercial programmes. The first solution has been adopted in the Argentine, in Mexico and in Uruguay ; in Bolivia, Peru, Guatemala and Nicaragua on the other hand, the official stations are also the principal commercial stations of the country. The authorities however have at their disposal appreciable revenue deriving from customs dues on all imports of radio material, from licences granted to broadcasters and radio amateurs, and also sometimes from a percentage on the advertising contracts of private stations.

But the main income of broadcasters is the sale of time which supports hundreds of stations and greatly contributes to the extension of broadcasting. Reaching millions of listeners, many of whom cannot read a newspaper, radio advertising is of very great importance for the national and also the inter-American economies.

There are a great many stations in Latin America : 900 transmitters, that is almost double the number in Europe and four times the number in Asia. But the power of these stations is generally very low and notwithstanding recent attempts to increase their radius of action by increasing their power, there yet remain (and probably will long remain) a multitude of small stations, using a few hundreds or even tens of watts and which elsewhere one would describe as amateur stations. Often these stations do not work according to a fixed time-table, but occasionally when they have advertising programmes to broadcast.

Alone the principal commercial societies—and sometimes the state—have sufficient means to build and run a high-power station. That is why there are in Latin America only 60 stations operating with a power of 10 to 40 kW and about 15 with 50 kW and more. Further it should be said that power is often reduced if the owner of the station is obliged to reduce his expenses, or increased when his business allows it ; it happens therefore that stations which two years ago worked with 100 kW or were authorized to use that much energy, now only use 5 and 10 kW and one of them even 500 Watts.

The situation is made more difficult by the lack of balance in the distribution of stations : the little transmitters which would have some right to exist if they were scattered over the whole of a country's territory are most often situated in a few towns. While Buenos-Ayres, Montevideo, Mexico City and other capitals have up to 25 and 30 stations and Havana even 40, there are vast regions entirely deprived of stations and insufficiently "covered". This inadequacy in the distribution is made worse by the almost complete absence of networks which could link the regional transmitters to central stations and ensure a wider reception of good programmes.

But the most remarkable phenomenon of Latin American broadcasting is the extraordinary development of transmission on short and intermediate waves ; their use allows the remotest regions to be reached and above all solves certain transmission problems which are particularly serious in the tropics. The number of stations using these frequencies has rapidly increased : from 13 in 1934 it has risen to about 245 at the present time [1].

---

[1] The activity of the 2,200 radio amateurs should be mentioned ; their stations are not infrequently transformed into commercial stations and occasionally give broadcast programmes.

The question of studios was long neglected and is still so today. Though there are transmitters of good technical quality the studio is often merely a room in the house of the owner of the station ; the modern auditoria are rare ; they are to be found, it appears, only in the Argentine, in Colombia and Uruguay.

Music predominates in all the programmes, however different they may be ; music is the essential element of every Latin American broadcast. It is given from morning till night, and some stations never broadcast anything else, being thus certain of winning the approval of the listeners who are passionately interested in national folklore. In order to send out so many musical programmes, the stations mostly use the gramophone records of which they have good collections. There is also great interest in the news, an interest which derives from the political enthusiasms of the people. The "Diario del Aire", broadcast several times a day, is completed by bulletins and commentaries relayed directly from abroad : as for special news, they are broadcast immediately they reach the station. Attention however is not entirely rivetted on politics ; information on stock exchange prices and especially news of sporting events are also listened to—any local, national or international competition is reported on the microphone.

Being so popular, music and news are the chosen instruments of advertising which is present everywhere, at all hours and in all programmes. Dozens of announcements (repeated several times during the day) are inserted between the records. The amount of direct publicity spoils the pleasure of listening and considerations of a commercial order often exert a bad influence on the standard and the composition of programmes ; the artistic and cultural side is too often neglected for the sake of concessions made to the taste of the masses. One must admit however that considerable progress has been achieved latterly, thanks to the gradual suppression of the abuses of commercial propaganda and thanks to the activity of the official services which are less dependent on popular approval. Their chief merit is the development of school broadcasting which has a real importance today. For about ten years Mexico alone offered educational programmes on a large scale. Today many Latin American states have special services for educational broadcasts on their own stations or at least have the use of a certain number of hours at the official stations. Following the American example, Porto Rico, Cuba, the Argentine, Uruguay and other countries have created Schools and Universities of the Air, which complement and continue school teaching. Special broadcasts have also been developed for the rural population and medical lectures to assist in the fight against tropical diseases and epidemics.

While fostering national art and national interests, the Latin American stations have always reserved a fairly important place for international programmes. From the beginning they have taken into account the existence of tens and hundreds of thousands of immigrants and their descendants and have organized for them "special hours" devoted to this or that nation, and announced in foreign languages. Numerous international relays, received from overseas through the big wireless telephone stations, enrich the local programmes, while certain short-wave stations, especially the official ones, endeavour to make the national culture known abroad. Finally the development of Pan-American broadcasting has greatly contributed—and will continue to do so—to the extension and improvement of programme material : hundreds of Latin American stations rebroadcast today programmes from the United States and try themselves to create programmes worthy of being heard in North America.

The question of reception is as important in Latin America as that of transmission. It is a serious problem for the authorities and the broadcasters, for still today a great many listeners are deprived of the pleasure of unhampered reception, on medium waves at least [1]. But in spite of all the difficulties, broadcasting enjoys great popularity. For the Latin American peoples are so fond of music and avid of news that they put up with the "inconveniences" of listening.

The number of receivers is as yet somewhat limited ; although it has doubled during the last few years, and even trebled in some countries, there are in this vast area—an area of 20,740,000 sq. km. and with 132,550,000 inhabitants—only

---

[1] For reasons of atmospherics, interference between the stations, electrical parasites, or on the other hand lack of electrification which necessitates the use of battery sets.

3 ½ to 4 million receivers. The number varies greatly in the different states : in the Argentine the million appears to have been surpassed ; in Mexico there are nearly 500,000 and in Brazil about 400,000 receivers ; in other countries, such as Guatemala, Costa Rica and Paraguay, the figures are 10 or 20 thousand and in others only a few thousands. Most sets are equipped for short-wave reception. The proportion of listeners per receiver is however much higher than in Europe and the United States ; in Mexico for instance the coefficient is estimated at seven and it is a certainty that collective listening greatly increases the numbers, for hundreds of listening posts are put up in the parks and the squares.

Some further details should be added on the countries which have the best developed services [1]. The first, Mexico, has no less than 151 medium-wave and 15 short-wave transmitters, among them the five most powerful stations of Latin America, licensed to operate with 100 or 150 kW [2]. Two chains have recently been formed, linked to the stations XEW and XEQ in Mexico City, the first with 23 stations. Some ten trans-mitters are managed by government departments and educational institutions ; the chief ones, however, all belong to commercial societies, whose advertising programmes are often directed (sometimes almost exclusively) to listeners in the United States. That is the reason for the numerous and powerful frontier stations which until latterly caused serious difficulties to American broadcasters [3]. Broadcasting in the Argentine is noteworthy thanks to its organization, its modern technical equipment, and its programmes, carefully

---

[1] Readers will find further details in our study "La Radiodiffusion en Amérique Latine", where a chapter is devoted to each country and which is being published in the *Journal des Télécommunications* (as from August 1941).

[2] Official list of stations dated October 1941. It no longer includes the famous station XERA Villa Acuña, of 180 kW (authorized to use 500 kW) ; this was confiscated on June 9, 1941 by order of the government for illicit political activity. cf. *Variety,* June 18, 1941, p. 35.

[3] Differences seem to have been smoothed over owing to energetic diplomatic intervention and the gradual application of the provisions of the Havana Treaty.

controlled by the authorities and far superior to those of most South American countries. The great majority of the 52 stations belong to private companies, whose annual receipts are over 13 million pesos. The two main ones are *Radio El Mundo* of 50 kW and *Radio Belgrano*, of 135 kW, serving as key-stations for chains of 11 and 9 stations. A third chain, affiliated to *Radio Splendid* recently increased from 16 to 50 kW, [1] is in process of formation and groups already 9 stations. The two 50 and 30 kW stations of the Municipality and the Provincial Government at Buenos Ayres also run on commercial lines. A special group consists of the four 10 kW transmitters of the State Broadcasting Service, whose activity is very fruitful.

Up to the present the situation of the radio in Brazil was confused and disorganized. But the government seems at last decided to take energetic measures to improve the service and to balance the excessively commercial activity of the 86 private stations (17 of which belong to radio clubs) by that of a group of official stations [2]. Already the authorities are endeavouring to fill in the lacunae in the programmes by broadcasting a daily national programme entitled "Hora do Brazil", for preference of an educational nature, and which all stations are obliged to relay free of charge.

Considerable progress has also been achieved in Peru whose government has entrusted the Marconi's Wireless Telegraph Company, Ltd. (which since 1921 has the monopoly of communications in that country) with the operation of the three official transmitters of 10 to 15 kW [3]. The same is true of Chile where 66 stations compete with one another, and of Colombia and Venezuela, each of which have about 75 transmitters, a large number of them using short or intermediate waves.

There are remarkable services in several small countries too, for instance in Uruguay. The *Servicio Oficial de Difusión*

---

[1] The energy of the station will shortly be increased to 100 kW.

[2] An important 50 kW short-wave centre, to be operated by the government, is now under construction.

[3] There are besides 19 small private stations.

Radio Electrica (SODRE) has since 1929 carried on a great artistic and cultural activity. It operates 6 stations and owns a group of modern studios at Montevideo ; it has formed the first symphony orchestra in the country, the first operatic company, and music schools which train collaborators for the radio. The example set by the national stations has stimulated the owners of the 46 private stations which multiply their efforts to improve their programmes. In Guatemala too the government is actively interested in the radio and very successfully operates 8 of the 10 stations. In Cuba on the other hand, it is the private stations—there are more than 100 of them !—that are very active, either independently or in affiliation with three networks each formed of seven to ten stations.

In the British colonies broadcasting stations and relay exchanges—generally controlled by the Governors—are closely linked to the BBC, many of whose programmes they carry. In the Dutch colony of Curaçao a listeners' association and a private service of wire broadcasting provide and distribute the programmes. In the French colonies all radio activity seems to have ceased and no station appears to be working since the outbreak of the war.

There is still much to be done before broadcasting in Latin America can render all the necessary services. But it is today at the beginning of a promising development.

III. Africa - Asia - Oceania

In the other parts of the world the development of broadcasting is somewhat irregular. Though a few countries possess services which are equal to the task, the majority have to be content with rather primitive services. It should however be admitted that the difficulties are enormous and that alone Japan and some of the British Dominions are able to overcome them. This is the more surprising that all countries, down to the most isolated islands, have today given the radio their allegiance and are preparing to organize regular services which will meet the national needs and even carry on a certain amount of international activity.

Africa

Of all the continents Africa is certainly the least favoured. Few of its countries are in a position to build stations, and fewer still have a sufficiently numerous non-native population to make the service pay. Notwithstanding recent progress, there are only 77 stations for a territory of 30 million square km !

French Protectorate

There are three main radio regions. In the first, that of the French Protectorate in North Africa, Algeria dominates more thanks to the work of the six stations than to their power which is limited to 10-12 kW for the main ones. Formerly operated by a managing association, *Radio-Alger* is now under the direct authority of the General Government of Algeria and the French national broadcasting service. War has postponed the plans for a 100 kW station, the building of which was already begun. The radio service is also very active in Morocco ; the principal station, founded in 1928, has been gradually reinforced from 2 to 25 kW and has recently had added to it two short-wave transmitters of 10 and 15 kilowatts. In Tunisia, where for a long time there were only two small private stations, the Post and Telegraph Administration opened on the eve of the war an official 20 kW station, broadcasting alternative programmes in French and Arabic. The financial regime of these protectorates is the same as in France : licence fees, and when necessary official subsidies. At the beginning of 1942 there were 111,900 receivers in Algeria, 49,000 in Morocco and 37,500 in Tunisia—relatively high figures, but which as yet only represent 15.47, 7.78 and 14.38 per thousand inhabitants.

* * *

Since October 1938 an important station of 50 kW is at work in Tripoli, chief town of Lybia, but its activity is not independent ; managed by the EIAR it relays first and foremost Italian programmes. It appears also that the chief aim of this station, too powerful for the needs of the colony, is to serve as an instrument of political propaganda.

Egypt

The second region is Egypt. The government was interested in the radio from early on and with the help of Marconi's Wireless Telegraph Company, Ltd. of London, created in 1926 the *Egyptian State Broadcasting Service.* The British society is responsible for the building and operation of the 6 stations which exist at present. A committee of three official delegates and two representatives of the company arrange the programmes. The main stations (Cairo I, of 20 kW, and Alexandria I of 1 kW) are especially used for broadcasts in Arabic, the alternative stations for European programmes. The number of licences, doubled in five years, was 86,477 at the beginning of 1941.

South Africa

The most important radio district is that of South Africa. Especially in the Union of South Africa, broadcasting is being fully developped under the aegis of the *South African Broadcasting Corporation (SABC)*, a public utility company founded in 1936 on the model of the BBC. Its function is to organize the service in the general interest ; although working closely with the government and responsible to Parliament, it is independent. British and Boer representatives and delegates from the different provinces sit on the board of directors appointed by the Governor General. Local councils also work in eight towns ; they are composed of well-known citizens and serve as links between the radio organization and the regional listeners. A special financial system takes into account the conditions of reception : the rather high licence fees (the average was 28 shillings 5d. in 1940) are graduated not only according to the usage (private or public) of receivers, but also according to the distance between listener and station [1].

---

[1] See our study "Les droits d'écoute dans le monde", *Journal des Télécommunications*, September 1939, p. 277.

The financial position of the Corporation is very good : in 1940 its revenue was £405,560 and the financial statement showed a profit of £75,000 notwithstanding rising expenditures.

The SABC has undertaken a complete reorganization of the service, formerly ruled by commercial considerations, in order better to cover the vast territory and satisfy the requirements of the two peoples living in the Union. The technical equipment of the network has been greatly enlarged and perfected so that the Corporation already operates 17 stations. A big broadcasting house has been built at Johannisburg with thirteen modern studios where two simultaneous programmes may be transmitted. Since 1937 alternative programmes are done in the two official languages, English and Afrikaans ; the latter are broadcast over short waves so as to reach the native populations, mostly living very far from the towns. But this bi-lingual service is in its intent always addressed to the whole nation. All broadcasting by political parties is strictly forbidden; so also is all commercial advertising. The extension of the service is considerable : in 1940 the South African stations did 67,630 hours of programmes (30,000 more than in 1937). At the same time the quality of the programmes has been much improved, especially the information service, school broadcasting, the educational lectures and the dramatic broadcasts. In order to cultivate good music, hitherto neglected in the Union, the Corporation has founded a big symphony orchestra in Johannesburg. It is the first in the country. Relations with the BBC have been constantly strengthened and the number of relays of British programmes, both news and artistic, ever increases. The interest of the public in the broadcasts is shown by the number of letters, which totalled 36,415 in 1939 and 177,548 in 1940, as well as in the increase in licences, rising from 131,424 when the official service was inaugurated to 283,119 at the beginning of 1941.

Similarly, the British colony of Kenya has had a broadcasting service since 1928, provided today by two small stations situated on a plateau at an altitude of 2,000 metres. It mostly offers local programmes and relays from Daventry. In spite of the relatively primitive nature of the service the radio is very popular in the colony and there are more than 5,000 receivers. In Southern Rhodesia the broadcasts have since 1932 been done by means of the two aeronautical stations of the post office. The service has been greatly developed, chiefly thanks to the help of the BBC, and now the formation of a proper radio organization is being planned ; the increase in licences, trebled between 1936 and 1939 (the number at present is about 12,000), serves as an encouragement for undertaking the preparatory work.

Other African territories also have small stations : the islands of Madagascar and Reunion, French Equatorial Africa—it is at Brazzaville that the transmitter of the Gaulliste forces works—the Belgian Congo, the Canary Islands, and especially Mozambique where a radio club owns nine short-wave transmitters. In several British colonies where there are no stations, as for instance the Gold Coast and Nigeria, there exist wire broadcasting services which relay the Daventry programmes. Finally, an important short-wave station was created several years ago in Addis Abeba, the capital of Ethiopia ; run by the Italian broadcasting society it had a power of 1 to 5 kW and used alternatively 18 short-wave frequencies. One may presume that the British authorities have put it into use.

Present events have endowed all these stations with a great importance—through them Europe speaks to the peoples of Africa ; further the stations are today called upon to keep the world informed of the fluctuations of battle.

Asia

For a long time Japan alone of the Asiatic countries was able to have its network of stations. But for five years now broadcasting in Asia has been in full swing, since many other countries are endeavouring to set up services. The main-spring of radio development is two-fold, political tendencies on the one hand, a desire to educate on the other. It is through the radio that Japan maintains and extends its influence, it is through the radio that China manifests her opposition, and it is the radio which links India to Great Britain. But it is above all education which is given through the radio, the rudiments of reading and writing being taught over the microphone.

Japan

Japan takes the lead in the continent of Asia. It instituted in 1926 [1] a big radio society : the *Nippon Hoso Kyokai* (Broadcasting Corporation of Japan), a non-commercial public service body, under the jurisdiction of the Ministry of Communications. A prince of the Imperial family is the "Protector" of the radio ; an influential committee composed of the vice-ministers of the six competent departments and of personalities representing various institutions or public authorities, decide on the programme policy ; finally some ten advisory committees participate in the organization of national or local broadcasts. The management is in the hands of a big Council, consisting of a president, the managing directors of the three "Divisions" (administration, technical and programmes), of numerous directors and inspectors.

The Corporation not only provides the broadcasting service, but, in order to raise the standard of manufacture, it also exercises a severe control over the radio industry. At the same time it undertakes the verification and free (!) repair of receivers so that good reception may be ensured.

The income largely depends on the licence fees which were gradually reduced from 12 to 9 and 6 Yens a year. This reduction was counterbalanced by an increase in the number of licences and led even to higher revenue, totalling 22,286,061 Yens in 1938/39 [2].

In three "five-year plan" stages the country was covered by central stations and relay-stations, forming a chain throughout the territory. The network now comprises 45 stations (excluding eight transmitters in Corea and five in Formosa) [3]. The two key-stations are Tokyo I and Tokyo II, of 150 kW each ; like the capital, Osaka and Nagoya have two transmitters, the second of which is reserved for the broadcasting of a purely educational programme. There is also in Tokyo an important short-wave centre with two 50 kW transmitters. The central

---

[1] With the help of 5,464 subscribers who contributed to the original fund.

[2] *Broadcasting in Japan*, yearbook published by the Nippon Hoso Kyokai, Tokyo, October 1939.

[3] *Ibidem*, p. 76 and 79.

stations each have two or three studios, those of Tokyo and Osaka even have spacious buildings, opened in 1939, and serving as headquarters for the Corporation.

The composition of programmes differs greatly from that in other countries. Recreational and artistic broadcasts are reduced to a minimum in favour of information and cultural education. 28.5% of all the programmes transmitted in 1938/39 by the Tokyo central stations were devoted to information, 23% to talks and lectures, and only 9% to musical broadcasts (527 hours in the whole year!) and 8.7% to entertainment [1]. The Japanese radio however shows great interest in the radio-theatre and the Tokyo station broadcasts some fifty drama programmes a month. Transmissions for foreign countries— at present seven separate programmes in 20 languages—are continually increased.

The radio endeavours to promote physical training in all ways possible. The whole year round, and three times a day, "radio-exercises" in which the whole nation participates, are broadcast. Every summer young and old meet in the open air, doing gymnastics to the commands of the loud-speaker. In 1939 there were 17,000 outdoor grounds equipped with "radio-towers" and 130 million participants [2]. Anxious to influence the populations of the Empire and the neighbouring countries, *Nippon Hoso Kyokai* works in close cooperation with the radio societies of Corea (*Tyosen Hoso Kyokai*), of Formosa (*Taiwan Hoso Kyokai*) and of Manchukuo (*Manchurian Telephone and Telegraph Company*), partly founded with Japanese capital ; the latter, which is very important, runs no less than 22 transmitters, the chief one at Hsinking of 100 kW [3]. Day by day the majority of Japanese programmes, transmitted over short waves, are relayed in these countries and in the occupied regions of China, Malaya and the Dutch East Indies ; many programmes are interchanged between the different organizations. With each new political advance, the Japanese radio extends its influence, always applying the principle of collaboration with the national services.

---

[1] *Broadcasting in Japan*, p. 23.

[2] *Ibidem*, pp. 33-34.

[3] *Ibidem*, p. 46.

The number of licences increases at a great pace and at the beginning of 1941 reached 5,369,898. But the density of receivers varies greatly in the different regions, in the towns and in the country : there are districts where most families have a radio set, there are others with only 10% or less. The interest aroused by present events adds to the attraction of radio and facilitates the intense political propaganda of the government.

China

Less authoritarian, China left (before the Sino-Japanese conflict) much freedom of action to the individual broadcasters, who were obliged merely to transmit the orders and communiqués of the government. Besides the private stations there were however many national stations in the hands of the public authorities (government or municipal) and educational institutions. The total was no less than 96 stations, the majority very weak ; 41 were situated in Shanghai ; but only one, the Nanking station XGOA of 75 kW, had any real importance.

The war has seriously affected the situation, dividing the country into two zones, one under the authority of the government of Chungking, the other under the control of the Japanese authorities and the new government in Nanking. In the first the Central Executive Committee of the Kuomingtang has developed an important radio organization, the *Central Broadcasting Administration*, with some 10 stations of which several are very powerful. The old transmitter of Nanking transferred to Chungking and working with a (provisionally reduced) power of 10 kW, serves as "central" station ; it is assisted by the two transmitters of the international station at Chungking of 35 kW, and a station of 60 kW in the province of Yunnan, as well as by several regional stations.

In occupied China the Japanese authorities have ceded to the new government the administration of a group of seven transmitters built and kept up by the Japanese army, especially at Shanghai, Nanking and Hankow [1]. An official society, the *Chinese Broadcasting Corporation*, placed under the

---

[1] *Cf. Bulletin, IBU*, May 1941, p. 137.

control of the Propaganda Department, was created to run
them ; the director of the new 20 kW station at Nanking is
assisted by a Japanese delegate. Another service has been
constituted in North-China ; the group of 11 transmitters is
headed by the stations of Peking and Tientsin.

The number of listeners is difficult to estimate ; official
indications and private information fluctuated (in 1937)
between 350,000 and 1 million ; at present it is estimated
that there are nearly 2 million receivers [1] but they reach a
much vaster audience since for several years every official
department, every office of the governing party, and every
school is obliged to possess a receiving installation accessible
to all the inhabitants.

India

Broadcasting in British India meets with great difficulties :
there are the geographic and climatic impediments, the many
peoples, speaking twenty different languages and innumerable
dialects, and the poverty of the majority of the population.
The stations were run at such heavy financial loss that their
suppression was considered. But in view of the role that the
radio is called upon to play in this country and in the life of the
353 millions inhabitants—mostly living in country districts
and frequently illiterate and ignorant of the rudiments of
hygiene—the Government of India in 1935 allocated the big
sum of 40,00,000 rupees [2] to the development of broadcasting.
It was thus possible to build a big station in New Delhi, soon
assisted by other important stations, and to create a national
service *All India Radio* (*AIR*).   It was put in charge of the
operation of the official stations and the control of broadcasts
over all territory under the authority of the central government [3]. A former official of the BBC was appointed "Controller
of Broadcasting" ; the central stations of each province are
under the management of competent directors with extensive
powers and great responsibilities. Regional advisory com-

---

[1] *Cf.* Dr. Tao Pung Fai, "Die Entwicklung des Rundfunks in
China", *Weltrundfunk*, April-May 1941, pp. 21-27.

[2] Equal to £300,000.

[3] The Native States are independent too where broadcasting is
concerned.

mittees, formed by the government, collaborate in the drawing up of programmes and maintain close contacts between the listeners and the central organs.

These efforts have been rewarded and the progress achieved in six years has surpassed all hopes : All India Radio operates today 15 transmitters (9 medium-wave and 6 short-wave), among them 4 in New Delhi, of 10 to 20 kW, and two of 10 kW in each of the other chief towns, Bombay, Calcutta and Madras. The formerly desperate financial situation has greatly improved today ; thanks to the growing interest of the public, the number of receivers and the imports of radio-electrical material have been increased, consequently raising the revenue from licence fees (10 rupees a year) and the customs duties. In four years the income of the service has thus been more than doubled and, notwithstanding growing expenditure, each of the recent financial periods has closed with an appreciable surplus.

The central stations each broadcast a different programme to which the intermediary transmitters add local features ; on one day a week each station must relay the programme of another. On the whole the programmes have a very definite national character ; they include however a number of European programmes, relayed mostly from the BBC Empire Station. The extent of the territory (4,684,298 sq. km.) and still more the divergent tastes and the many languages oblige the radio both to multiply and decentralize its activities ; the four Delhi stations for instance must every day transmit 77 news bulletins in seven Indian languages, in English and in Persian. All India Radio must also devote very special attention to listeners in the rural districts since they are most in need of broadcasts, but lack the money to buy receivers. Consequently collective listening with receivers distributed free prevails. Following on the first experiments made in 1938 the authorities have set up hundreds of receivers in remote villages, often 300 miles away from the central stations. Here as elsewhere the rural and the educational radio supplement each other making up for the absence of educational institutions.

The governments of the Native States are following the example of the Government of India and, more and more desirous of introducing the radio on their territories, devote considerable sums to the establishment and development of regular broadcasting services. Stations have been built by the authorities in Baroda, Hyderabad, Travancore, and also by the Burma Posts and Telegraph Department.

After years of crisis and vain endeavour broadcasting in British India has at last achieved success. The programmes are enthusiastically welcomed and there is a big increase of licences, from 10,000 at the beginning of 1934 to 50,000 in 1937 and 130,461 in the spring of 1941. Everything seems to indicate that this movement in favour of broadcasting will steadily continue.

There is also an excellent service in Ceylon where an official station was put up as early as 1925 in Colombo. Operating at present with 4 kW, its range of activity is far greater than that of a small colonial station ; it broadcasts up to 3,000 programmes a year and such is its success that between 1935 and 1939, the number of licences was almost trebled, going from 2,342 to 6,013. In Hongkong, too, the colonial government had created a well organized service, broadcasting (before the Japanese occupation) on medium and short waves alternative European and Chinese programmes, received on the 12,000 sets in the colony. The development of the radio was less auspicious in Malaya where circumstances have begun to improve only since 1938. Three organizations at Singapore, Penang and Kuala Lumpur were responsible for the five small stations, working for approximately 12 to 15,000 listeners. All these transmitters have been taken over by the Japanese authorities and work under their control.

Recent events also affect broadcasting in the Philippines which were closely linked to the mother-country. The regime was the same as that in the United States : management was entirely in private hands and the five stations [1]—two of which were affiliated to the NBC—derived their income from the sale of time. Several days before the fall of Manila, all stations were "dismantled and destroyed" by their owners.

---

[1] Each with two transmitters, operating one on medium and one on short waves.

Mention must also be made of broadcasting in Thailand where four official stations have been working for many years in Bangkok, and in French Indo-China where there are three private short-wave stations, the most important of 12 kW at Saïgon.

Dutch East Indies

In the Dutch East Indies broadcasting developed (until 1940) in close connection with Holland. A private company, the NIROM [1], created in 1934 a regular service receiving its instructions from Amsterdam. Following the example of the broadcasting associations in the mother-country, it secured a big influence for listeners, giving them 10 out of the 14 seats on the Programme Committee. Levying a heavy licence fee (beginning with 30 florins, but gradually reduced to 18 florins), the society set up numerous short or intermediate-wave stations throughout the territory ; these were fed with the programmes of the central stations of Batavia, Bandoeng and Surabaya and (before the invasion of the Netherlands) with relays from the Dutch short-wave stations. There were besides some 20 local listeners' associations and radio clubs with their own little transmitters. Thus in 1941 there were 48 stations of which the two main ones had 5 and 10 kW. To prevent the stations from falling into the hands of the Japanese troops, the principal transmitters were destroyed or heavily damaged. Only in April 1942 could the service be resumed and programmes be relayed from Tokyo. The number of receivers increased steadily : 39,000 at the beginning of 1937 it is now over 110,000.

Palestine

There has also been remarkable progress in broadcasting in the Near East, above all in Palestine which, though one of the youngest of the radio countries, has succeeded in developing in five years an official service of a high standard. The radio is at the same time the voice of Great Britain and the mediator between populations so different and so much in opposition

---

[1] *Nederlandsch-Indische Radio Omroep Maatschappij.*

to each other. These conditions determine the work of the *Palestine Broadcasting Service* which runs a 20 kW station near Jerusalem ; it is financed by a licence fee of 750 Mils (about 15 shillings) and limited advertising.

The programmes are extremely difficult to arrange since they have to be broadcast in the three official languages— English, Hebrew and Arabic—and since it is necessary to take into account the reactions of an audience made up of immigrants from many nations. But the listeners have one point in common—love of music. In all circles musical program- mes meet with an enthusiastic welcome. Much work is done in the domains of educational and rural broadcasting with the help of the University of Jerusalem and the Department of Agriculture ; collective listening is organized, especially in the Arab villages. Licences numbered 12,200 when the service was opened, and touched 50,000 in 1940 ; they are mostly held by Jewish listeners, the Arabs having only several thousands of private sets.

* * *

Two new official services were created in 1940 in Iran and in Afghanistan ; *Radio-Teheran* operates an important station with two transmitters, one of 2 kW (medium waves) and one of 25-32 kW (short-wave), whilst the Ministry of Communications at Kabul works a 20 kW station located near the capital at a height of 2,000 metres [1]. Finally in Irak, there are two small transmitters which will be replaced by a big station at Baghdad working with 5 and 20 kW on nine medium, intermediate and short wavelengths [2].

The recent development of broadcasting, the opening of new services, the improved programmes and the increase in the number of listeners had given grounds to hope that very good progress might be made. But today broadcasting in Asia—so much in need of a long period of normal and steady development—is subjected to the conflict of armies, and other duties take precedence over education which should be the chief aim of the radio in this part of the globe.

---

[1] *Cf. Weltrundfunk* 1941, No. 1-2.

[2] List of Broadcasting Stations 1940, supplement No. 1, August 9, 1941. Int. Telecommunication Union.

OCEANIA

However curious it may seem, Oceania—the part most distant from the centres of radio electrical development—has from the first taken an interest in broadcasting. Under the influence of Great Britain and the impulse given by an important industrial firm [1], the two British Dominions have been able to create a remarkable service covering the entire region of the Pacific and able to counter-balance other influences coming from Asia.

Australia

The difficulties encountered by broadcasting in Australia are the same as in other Dominions : geographical hindrances due to the size of the country (7,703,387 sq. km.), regional differences increased by the political system of the Commonwealth which consists of six autonomous states. Yet the linguistic unity and the happy cooperation between the authorities and the private broadcasters have done much to render possible the creation of a huge network across the whole continent.

The foundations of the present system were laid already in 1924 by a regulation dividing the stations into two groups : Class A, financed by licence fees, and Class B, dependent for its revenue on the sale of time for advertising purposes. Five years later the government bought the stations of the first group and inaugurated the *National Broadcasting Service.* The Postmaster-General reserved for himself the technical side and entrusted the Australian Broadcasting Company with the programmes ; the latter was replaced in 1932 by the *Australian Broadcasting Commission (ABC)* which enjoys a good deal of independence. The Commission is composed of 5 to 7 members, assisted by a Director General [2]. On every licence

---

[1] The Amalgamated Wireless Australasia Ltd. (AWA), which organized in 1920 the first demonstrations of broadcasting in Sydney.

[2] For some time a project of reorganization has been studied which however does not envisage the modification of the regime but would only tend to increase the Commission's means for action and would also hand over the technical services to it.

fee—of 15 or 21 sh.—twelve shillings go to the Commission, the rest to the Postal Department. Thanks to the success of the national broadcasts the revenue of the ABC has increased from year to year ; for the financial year 1939/40 its share of licences was £700,071 to which must be added £73,794 derived from other sources, especially public concerts. Total expenses at the time were £726,611 of which 78.84% was devoted to programmes [1].

The Class B stations belong mostly to commercial compagnies and derive their income from radio advertising which annually brings in £1,000,000. The most important of these is the *Amalgamated Wireless Australasia, Ltd.* (AWA), a radio manufacturing society owning four medium-wave and three short-wave stations. A certain number of transmitters belong to private broadcasters, to newspapers, or to religious groups.

Since the creation of the official Commission, the Australian radio has made tremendous progress. The number of stations increased to 129 : 29 national stations (Class A), forming a chain of about 4,000 miles, and 100 private stations (Class B). In each capital of the Australian states—Sydney, Melbourne, Brisbane, Adelaide, Perth and Hobarth—the national service has two stations and is thus able to broadcast alternative programmes. Five stations operate on short waves, not only for foreign countries but also for Australian listeners in far-off regions. A few years ago practically all the stations were very weak ; today there are already about 15 official stations of 7 to 10 kW. The power of commercial stations is in principle limited to 2 kW and only two short-wave stations of the AWA—intended for intercontinental transmissions—possess higher power, that of Melbourne, 5 kW, and that of Sydney, 16 kW ; at the present time the latter is partly reserved for broadcasts by the Department of Information. Numerous private transmitters have grouped themselves into networks in order to increase their range and to reinforce their advertising possibilities. Thus 24 stations are affiliated to the Commonwealth Broadcasting Network and 19 to the Marquarie Broadcasting Services. For very special transmissions intended for the whole nation, official and

---

[1] Annual Report of the ABC, Sydney 1940.

private stations form a single chain which is then composed of 100 to 120 stations [1].

The programmes keep pace with technical progress. They steadily increase in number and improve in quality. During 1939/40 their total duration was 149,855 hours, or 668,510 programmes! Every day one "national programme" (to which every state contributes) is transmitted to the whole continent besides the "regional programmes" organized by the various states and making use of local talent.

The entire activity of the Australian Broadcasting Commission is influenced by the desire to contribute to the cultural progress of the Dominion—an extremely difficult task in a country, some parts of which are a desert and which is so far away from the centres of artistic and intellectual life in the European and American continents. It has been necessary to discover and to develop the local artistic talent, bring the various organizations into fruitful collaboration with each other and create everywhere new cultural groups, for instance several symphony orchestras numbering 50 to 90 performers. Thanks to the ABC the Australian public is able to hear each season numerous artists of world renown and enjoy opera. The radio has helped to foster the development of an artistic movement which manifests itself by an increasing interest in serious music. But the national service is also keenly interested in the radio-theatre, which is appreciated in few countries as much as it is in Australia, in lectures which always figure largely in the programmes, in school broadcasting which is a great favourite with all listeners—not only the young. The news service is extremely important in so big a country and the ABC has constantly enlarged it in collaboration with two important press agencies and with local newspapers. Among the most popular programmes which excite passionate interest must be mentioned the cricket broadcasts. Every time the Australian team visits England, tens of thousands of Australians buy radio sets in order to be able to follow the special transmissions organized for the occasion.

---

[1] The transmission of a message by the Prime Minister, organized with the help of 150 engineers, had necessitated the use of 18,000 miles of telephone lines.

The relations between the Australian commission and the British Broadcasting Corporation are very close and have become yet closer since the outbreak of the war. The national stations regularly relay certain British programmes and every Sunday they give a "BBC Hour" in order that Australian listeners may participate in the activity of the English radio. In turn Australia plays an important part in the Empire broadcasts and produces very interesting programmes.

Like the national ones, the private stations are very active. Some of them work from 6 a.m. till midnight and one of them even provides a 24 hour service. Entertainment and recorded programmes are most prominent ; the AWA has therefore created a centre where annually thousands of programmes are produced and recorded [1].

Thanks to the great increase in licences, Australia holds today a special place as regard the number of receivers as well as their density. Three years ago the first million was reached and at the end of June 1940 1,212,580 out of the 6,866,590 inhabitants possessed receiving sets, *i.e.*, 173.3 per thousand. In certain regions this proportion is even greater and reaches the figure of 200 in South Australia.

* * *

Spreading from Australia, the radio has also reached the territories of Papua (British New Guinea) and even the Fiji Islands, where it is of the greatest service to officials and lonely settlers. The Amalgamed Wireless Australasia has here and there built stations which it operates.

New Zealand

For many years broadcasting in New Zealand followed lines of development parallel with the Australian. The same distinction was made between national stations, run by a programme council, and private stations, belonging to commer-

---

[1] One of the commercial companies had before the war acquired the exclusive right to broadcast the recorded programmes of "Radio-Luxembourg".

cial societies and radio clubs, eight of which even regularly received government subsidies. Yet the government exercised stricter control over the commercial stations and gradually the influence of the state has become stronger, culminating in the suppression of an advisory programme committee and, finally, of the Council itself. In 1936 the authorities created a new radio organization, the *National Broadcasting Service*. Henceforth the government had a direct control over all broadcasting activities, official as well as private. It even bought up numerous small transmitters and added to the national service a *Commercial Broadcasting Service*, giving an alternative programme and living not from the proceeds of licences but from advertising. Today the first group comprises 17 stations, the most important of which are Wellington 2YA, of 60 kW, heard over the whole territory, and the principal stations of Auckland, Christ Church and Dunedin, of 10 kW each. The commercial service owns in each of these towns a 1 kW station, and in addition a small relay station ; it has also a station on wheels—a railway van belonging to the National Railways, equipped with a 250 Watt transmitter and a studio with all the necessary control apparatus. (Since the autumn of 1940 the two networks are closely linked together and work in perfect synchronization). Finally there are some small private stations which broadcast commercial programmes only.

At Auckland there is a big broadcasting house and the other broadcasting centres were to be given similar equipment. Wellington was to be endowed with a splendid auditorium similar to Broadcasting House in London. Though it has not been possible to carry out this plan owing to the war, it has by no means been abandoned.

The financial position of the National Service is very good ; the proceeds of the annual licence fee of 25 shillings fully cover the expenditure, high though it is. In 1939, it already had a reserve fund of £557,522. As for the commercial service, the government had to invest important sums in it and it was only after some years that the running of it became profitable.

With the increase in the number of national stations and the extension of the programmes, the length of broadcasting time has also considerably increased and in 1940 reached 52,818 hours. As does the Australian radio, so the New Zealand service promotes school broadcasting and offers a great many special programmes [1] to over 1,100 schools. The news service is no less developped—since the beginning of the war, the national stations have organized a continuous service in order to give to their listeners all the news from Europe as soon as it is received.

A special feature of the New Zealand radio is the regular transmission of the parliamentary debates enabling the inhabitants of the Dominion to follow closely the activity of their representatives. Each session is broadcast in its entirety by two national stations without any attempts at political propaganda being made in favour of one or other of the parties. The success of these broadcasts which were first planned as an experiment but which have now been going on for four years is extraordinary : the debates in parliament are a general topic of conversation ; the broadcasting of the discussions has a good influence on the politicians and on their speeches ; furthermore the nation takes a great interest in public affairs and realizes better the difficult task of those who govern [2].

The commercial service tries to complete the rather serious programmes of the national stations by entertainment ; it also organizes a large number of non-commercial programmes, in particular special broadcasts for specific regions or specific groups of listeners.

The number of licences has been increasing regularly during the past six years by 30,000 to 50,000 per annum ; on January 1, 1941 the total was 352,055. As regards density, New Zealand with 212.1 sets per thousand inhabitants is the fourth country in the world and it is expected that saturation point will shortly be reached.

Hawaii Islands

The voice of the Islands of Hawaii is also heard in the Pacific. Since 1922 this American colony has adopted broad-

---

[1] At the time of an epidemic of infantile paralysis, the radio took on the work of teaching and transmitted regular lessons to the pupils of the schools which were closed.

[2] *Cf. World Radio*, London, August 19, 1938 p. 7.

casting and the first station, KGU Honolulu, is proud to have obtained one of the first licences. Today there are four stations, one of 5 kW and the others of 2.5 kW. They are operated independently and run on big advertising which brings in very large sums, especially since three stations are affiliated to the USA networks. This also explains the great success of the programmes and the unhoped-for increase in receivers : 20,000 in 1935, they now number about 50,000. The Hawaiian service is in a way symbolic of the nature of broadcasting, linking the colonies to the mother-country and islands to continents.

IV. INTERNATIONAL SERVICES AND BROADCASTING ORGANIZATIONS

"Radio-Nations" and "Radio-Vaticana"

The example of the BBC and its "Empire Service" which, since 1932, has carried out short-wave transmissions for overseas listeners, has been followed by many other broadcasting companies. That period has also witnessed the creation of two international services : "Radio-Nations" and "Radio-Vaticana".

In order to guarantee independent and direct communications with most of its members, the League of Nations inaugurated in 1932, at Prangins, a station called *Radio-Nations* composed of one long-wave transmitter for wireless telegraphy and two 20 kW short-wave transmitters for wireless telephony and broadcasting. In times of crisis its operation, which was in normal times entrusted to the wireless telegraph and telephone company "Radio-Suisse", was to be exclusively in the hands of the League[1]. The Secretariat organized its programmes : weekly bulletins in English, French and Spanish, and special broadcasts of the meetings of the Assembly, of Commissions as well as speeches and messages by eminent personalities. Frequently the International Labour Office also used the station and broadcast information on its activity, speeches by its Director and by delegates to the Labour Conference.

---

[1] According to the clauses of the agreement signed on May 21, 1929 between the Swiss Government and the League of Nations.

The creation of "Radio-Nations" aroused hopes which were unfortunately not fulfilled. At all times the service was seriously hampered by the fact that it could never broadcast on long and medium waves except through the intermediary of national stations. Thus the League broadcasts reached only the countries outside Europe and, in those, only the owners of short-wave sets—a state of affairs quite inconceivable for such an institution. But what is even worse, "Radio-Nations" had to stop its regular programmes at the beginning of hostilities—at the very moment when its voice was more than ever necessary. Since September 1939, the station has only given occasional programmes such as those organized at the closing and re-opening of the League Pavilion at the New York World's Fair. Contrarily to the original provisions, it was not the Secretariat but the company "Radio-Suisse" which continued to operate the station used for commercial communications and the transmission of programmes for the Swiss living abroad as well as for the relays of some American broadcasting companies. On February 2 1942 the contracts between the Federal Council and the Radio-Suisse S.A. on the one part and the League of Nations on the other part were cancelled ; the company which had shared in the costs of setting up "Radio-Nations" bought back all the equipment belonging to the League of Nations [1]. Thus the station has become wholly Swiss and henceforth the voice of the League of Nations is silent.

The Lateran Treaty of 1929 enabled the Holy See to create its own radio centre in the Papal State. To the wireless tele-graph and telephone station, opened in 1941, was added some time later an important short-wave broadcasting station, *Radio-Vaticana* of 25 kW. Conceived and carried out by Senator Marconi, it began to operate to full capacity in 1934. The absence of a medium-wave channel was never so serious here as it was in the case of the League of Nations station, since the Vatican—much more so than a political institution—finds national stations prepared to relay its programmes [2]. Its numerous bulletins and talks are mostly of a religious character, include liturgical commentaries and spiritual

---

[1] *cf.* Rapport de Gestion 1941 de "Radio-Suisse", S.A. de Télé-graphie et Téléphonie sans fil, May 27, 1942.

[2] A Christmas concert for example was relayed in 13 European countries and in 15 countries in America.

guidance, and now also information on the prisoners of war. Special broadcasts sent throughout the world are given on the occasion of Pontifical Mass at the time of great festivities, Canonisation Ceremonies, Eucharistical Congresses, and Papal Benedictions and Messages. The war has in no way interrupted the activities of the station which on the contrary has increased the number and the duration of its daily programmes and now speaks in ten languages.

International Broadcasting Organizations

Never would so much progress have been realized either in technique or in programmes without the continuous and friendly collaboration of broadcasters or without the international organizations devoted to broadcasting. It is this collaboration which has made it possible to find a general solution to a multitude of problems and has thus saved broadcasting from the chaos which threatened its development in its early years.

The most important of these organizations is the *International Broadcasting Union (IBU)* founded in April 1925 in Geneva by the government administrations and broadcasting services of nine European countries[1]. The Union, unlike most international organizations, consists of official, semi-official as well as private organizations. It has three categories of membership[2] :

1. Full members—State services or those created by the State, private societies or enterprises operating a broadcasting service in a country of the European zone under the authority or with the permission of the competent Administration ;

2. Associate members—broadcasters or groups of broadcasters operating a service outside the European zone ;

3. Special members—broadcasting organizations working under a special regime (for instance, the Vatican).

---

[1] Austria, Belgium, France, Germany, Great Britain, the Netherlands, Poland, Spain and Switzerland.

[2] *Cf.* Statutes of the IBU, and Arthur R. Burrows "The International Broadcasting Union", Sept. 4, 1939.

The Council consists of the president, four vice-presidents and a representative for each European country. The work of the Union is done through the International Broadcasting Office at Geneva, under the direction of the Secretary General of the Union[1], the International Checking Centre at Brussels and four Committees of specialists entrusted with the study of technical problems, of programmes and international relays as well as with legal and budgetary questions. Created at first to deal with a technical crisis, the IBU soon took on other tasks and became a centre of study and research for all problems connected with broadcasting.

It is in the technical domain that the most startling results were obtained. The studies were the basic material for an international discussion for the purpose of setting up plans for the allocation of wave lengths. In addition, the IBU, by its Checking Centre created in 1927 and wittily called "Police of the Air", controls the use of frequencies and the stability of broadcast transmitters. Every day measurements are taken of hundreds of wavelengths—an average of 500 in the spring of 1942—and any inaccuracy is immediately brought to the attention of the station in question. Thus is has often been possible to eliminate in less than two hours serious disturbances and gradually to suppress interferences which sometimes affected millions of listeners. At the time of the invasion of Belgium, the engineers of the Centre, in order to preserve the valuable equipment from possible destruction, evacuated the control apparatus and brought it safely to Geneva, where the service was set up at the Palais Wilson in the premises of the Office. A few months later however the equipment was returned to Brussels where the Centre continues to function, *ad interim* under the direction of a German expert.

In the field of programmes the activity of the Union, and more particularly of its Office in Geneva, was no less important. It is to it that we owe the development of the system of exchange of programmes and performers between nations and continents. Broadcasters had hoped that it might lead to a *rapprochement* of the peoples. International relays of important musical, sporting and national events were organized as well as

---

[1] *Ad interim* the Secretary General of the Swiss Broadcasting Service.

transmissions with the collaboration of many stations, especially at Christmas time, the New Year and on other occasions [1] ; the National and European Concerts were succeeded in 1936 by the World Concerts which were transmitted simultaneously in the five continents.

A large number of publications testify to the activity of the Union. Hundreds of graphics show the frequency measurements taken by the Checking Centre ; the monthly bulletins published now in five languages and numerous other documents inform the members of the development of broacasting, of the latest methods of organization, of important decrees and the newest technical improvements.

A true "League of Broadcasters", the Union has had a tremendous development and has in turn had considerable influence on broadcasting. Grouping at first only nine societies —owning 50 stations with a total power of 60 kW—its membership was over 60 on the eve of the war, including the majority of European services and the most important organizations in America, Africa, Asia and Oceania. The number of its stations was then about 900 with a total power of over 12,000 kW ; and their programmes could be heard by at least 300 million listeners.

The war is for the Union a hard test and lessens its activities. The suppression of numerous organizations, as for instance in the Netherlands, in Poland, in the Baltic countries and in Jugoslavia, has greatly reduced the membership of the Union ; the resignation of Great Britain, a founder-member, has moreover led to the resignation of Palestine and of several Dominions [2]. But the services rendered in the past are so great that it is generally desired to maintain the IBU. A meeting of its Council clearly indicated the will of national services to keep their international organization to serve as a link between the countries and the broadcasters.

Following the lines and the statutes of the IBU, the broadcasting groups of South America formed in 1934 the *Union Sudamericana de Radiodifusión (USARD)*. Created to satisfy

---

[1] The 1935 world transmission "Youth Sings over the Frontiers", used children's choirs from thirty-one countries and was relayed by 400 stations.

[2] *Cf. Bulletin IBU* February 1942 and *Journal des Télécommunications* June 1942.

technical needs, its first aim was to establish a plan of allocation for the continent. But it had yet other tasks to perform ; it tried to contribute to the betterment of the programmes, to the exchange of publications and of information. Above all it saw to it that the pledge to avoid any broadcast which might harm the good relations between the contracting countries was carried out. For some time now preparatory conversations have been taking place between the broadcasters of the two Americas with a view to grouping all the radio services in a great Pan American Broadcasters' Union [1].

* * *

Other groups with more limited objects deal with certain aspects of broadcasting. Thus the *Comité International de Radioélectricité* (*C.I.R.*), created in 1922 with headquarters in Paris, and dealing before the war with the study of juridical and economic questions, had a membership of some 30 national committees.

The pioneers of Catholic broadcasting founded in 1928 a central organ, the *Bureau Catholique International de la Radiodiffusion* (*B.C.I.R.*) ; its offices were transferred in 1936 from Düsseldorf to Amsterdam. Comprising representatives of more than 30 nations in and outside Europe, it was the centre of all Catholic broadcasting activities. Through its delegates and with the help of ecclesiastical authorities and catholic associations, it endeavoured to achieve a higher moral and spiritual level in programmes.

Of more recent date (1936) but by no means negligible is the *Centre International de Radiophonie Rurale* (*C.I.R.R.*) in Rome, created under the auspices of the "Fédération Internationale des Techniciens Agronomes".

Its Board of Directors is made up exclusively of specialists for agricultural questions and rural broadcasting. A centre of documentation and information, it has held world-wide inquiries on the methods and the effects of the agricultural radio [2].

---

[1] Statement by John F. Royal, vice-president of NBC, in *Pan American Radio ; cf.* also *Journal des Télécommunications*, January 1942, p. 17.

[2] The results were published in the international bulletin of the CIRR, entitled *Radiophonie Rurale*.

Today these three organizations are "marking time", all direct action having become impossible under present conditions. But once peace is restored they will certainly take up their work immediately.

An organ of the League of Nations has also dealt with radio questions : the *International Institute of Intellectual Cooperation*. First it made a study of the problems of school broadcasting and of the intellectual value of programmes [1] ; then it examined the possibilities of using radio broadcasting in the interests of peace [2] and prepared the international convention adopted in 1936 in Geneva [3]. But it was already too late ; though many countries had agreed to this convention, though some had begun to give effect to its recommendations, it was too late to prevent the War on Waves.

---

[1] *School Broadcasting*, Paris 1933 ; *The Educational Role of Broadcasting*, Paris 1935.

[2] *Broadcasting and Peace*, Paris 1933.

[3] "International Convention concerning the Use of Broadcasting in the Cause of Peace".

C.   NEW DEVELOPMENTS

Twenty years of progress and of astonishing achievement
have conferred tremendous power on broadcasting—it has
entered our homes, it forms part of our daily life. Nevertheless,
as an American broadcaster has said, the radio is still in its
"infancy" and "real progress is still to come". It surely will
come and will even be hastened by the war. For if today
we witness the destruction of services built up and developed
with so much labour and patience, stations to which we were
wont to listen every evening, it is none the less true that the
use of radio equipment for war purposes stimulates its technical
improvement and gives birth to new inventions. And while
the state, on the plea of the exigencies of national defence,
today takes over so many broadcasting stations, it is certain
that private initiative will revive with forces the greater for
having been kept so long in check.

The complete state control of the services, as applied today
in certain countries, can hardly be permanent. For experience
has shown that it is desirable to find the balance between private
initiative and official control, both of which are necessary
for the growth and development of broadcasting. Laws which
are too rigid are contrary to the very nature of the radio and
deprive it of its wonderful possibilities ; unbounded liberty
however merely leads to chaos which thwarts normal
progress and from which it is the listener who suffers.

The solution of the problems of organization will in large
measure depend on the outcome of the war. Future technical
devices, however, seem more probable, since they derive from
the laws of science and no political or military decision can
modify them. The most urgent task which will certainly be
undertaken on the cessation of war is the setting up of a
new allocation plan for wave lengths in the European zone.
The "Montreux Plan" adopted shortly before the war, may
serve as a basis ; for its premises and suggestions, if not all

its stipulations, remain valid [1]. Then, and without delaying too long, it will be necessary to establish that world plan for short waves for which broadcasters and listeners in the whole world are eagerly waiting and which is vital for the future development of international broadcasting.

Other important changes of a national and regional character will also no doubt occur and the way has already been prepared for them. New networks will be made or the existing ones renovated in countries hitherto inadequately provided for—in the Balkans, in the Near East and in Latin America. Short-wave centres will be enlarged and new ones created in Denmark, Hungary, Slovakia, Portugal, the Argentine, Brazil, and especially in the United States. More and more will the practice be extended of building stations with two or three transmitters broadcasting (as in London and Florence) simultaneous programmes or working (as do many Latin American stations) on different frequency bands, on long, short or intermediate waves. Finally "the race for power", begun twelve years ago, is not likely to stop as yet; it is indeed extending to the domain of short waves. Almost everywhere the building of powerful stations of 100 and 120 kW is being undertaken or planned, in Slovakia, Croatia and Rumania, in the Argentine, Mexico, Algeria, Morocco, Japan and Australia. And it is not beyond the range of possibilities that the present power limit of 500 kW will soon be surpassed. The requests for permits made by certain American stations clearly suggest this. Among the important plans for the future is included the construction of many modern studios and buildings in the Netherlands, in Denmark, in some of the Balkan countries, in India, Australia and New Zealand, but especially in several Latin American states.

Where programmes are concerned, many problems await solution. Balance has not yet been achieved between the various types of programmes, between the light and the serious. Broadcasting, formerly too casual, has become too dramatic, agitated, reflects too closely our troubled times.

---

[1] See Raymond Braillard "Les bases techniques du Plan de Montreux", *Journal des Télécommunications*, February 1941, pp. 25-35.

Instead of attracting us, it thrusts itself upon us, and the passion for propaganda at all hours and in all kinds of forms, causes the potential enrichment of our lives to be neglected. But the efforts of the pioneers of the radio—saddened today by the deformation of their work [1]—are not entirely lost. They will be taken up again where they have been left ; once again there will be a happy collaboration between broadcasters of all nations. The need of such a revival is making itself felt again ; this is shown by the increasingly frequent exchanges between allied and friendly countries and by the development of the Pan American broadcasting. The scaffolding is ready ; the tools are there. The international radio organizations are impatiently waiting for the day when they will be able to regain their freedom of action. But there is yet lacking that big international broadcasting centre, which is neither at the service of one state nor of one organization, but at the service of all the forces fighting for the betterment of humanity. Utopian today, it should be possible to create it tomorrow and that will be one of the first tasks of the post-war time. But it is to be hoped that the lesson of that disappointing experiment "Radio-Nations" will have been learnt.

The "war on waves" and more particularly the mass broadcasting of propaganda have in many countries led to the restriction or even suppression of that freedom of listening which broadcasters and listeners had long considered as a sacred right. If, at the end of war, the broadcasts of all countries become, as one hopes, once again accessible to all peoples, one lesson gleaned from the political radio will have to be remembered. That is the possibility of organizing collective listening and thus securing the attention of the masses. That experience can and must be applied to good purpose, for mass instruction and education. But, if it is not to fail in its task, broadcasting must first of all train its listeners to a more ordered, more ponderate way of listening. For one of its worse enemies is the listener who turns on the wireless at any time

---

[1] The illustrious American inventor Dr. Lee de Forest for instance has protested against the present-day use of the radio which he had destined for the work of peace and the improvement of human relationships.

without really paying attention, who every day "swallows"
dozens of programmes without having chosen a single one,
for whom the radio broadcast is merely a "background noise".
Many broadcasters are today aware of this failing and a radio
review severely condemns it [1].

* * *

All these problems, however important they may be, fade in
comparison with the prospects opened up today by the use
of ultra-short waves (from 1 to 10 metres) and the new radio
discoveries :   Frequency   Modulation   Broadcasting   (FM),
Facsimile Service and Television [2].   Causing revolutionary
changes in transmission and in reception, they will exercise
a decisive influence on future developments.   For each offers
vast possibilities and advantages which justify its introduction
and guarantee its success.

Frequency Modulation Broadcasting especially is at the
present time in great favour in the United States.   Introduced
in 1936 by Major Edwin H. Armstrong, that method of transmission has developed so rapidly that it might well banish one
day the usual method of amplitude modulation broadcasting [3].
Experiments yielded conclusive results ; it has been proved that
FM offers a solution to the problem of "static" [4], allows natural

---

[1] The *ABC Weekly*, official organ of the National Australian
Service, January 10, 1942.

[2] Our study being confined to broadcasting today, it is impossible
to examine in detail the radio devices of tomorrow.   We therefore
recommend to readers interested in these questions the special
number of "*The Annals*", January 1941, entitled "New Horizons
in Radio", containing excellent non-technical articles by well-
known American experts.

[3] The   term   "frequency   modulation"   means   a   system   of
modulation of a radio signal in which the frequency of the carrier
wave is varied in accordance with the signal to be transmitted
while the amplitude of the carrier remains constant.   (Rules
Governing FM, adopted by the FCC, June 22, 1940, Sec. 3,203).
The technical processes are described in a paper presented by
Major Armstrong to the Institute of Engineers, November 1935.

[4] This term includes all disturbances produced by natural causes,
e.g., lightning storms, or man-made causes, working of electrical
machinery.

sound reproduction and, since it opens new bands in the ultra-high frequency region (over 30,000 kc), can provide channel space for thousands of stations. For the ultra-short waves have a limited range and one may without fear of interference allocate the same frequency to a station in a neighbouring region. In May 1940, FM broadcasting was officially recognized, the Federal Communications Commission having admitted its value and importance authorized the commercial operation of FM transmitters and reserved for them 35 high-frequency channels. Since then requests for licences pour into the FCC, which had up to January 1942 authorized 62 commercial and 16 educational or experimental FM stations. The first twenty-four commercial transmitters, run mostly by standard broadcast stations, are in use and work on a regular schedule ; the others are being built. Some have high power (50 kW), and the formation of networks, whose stations will be linked by radio and not by telephone lines, is even contemplated. Moreover owing to its characteristics and advantages, FM is extremely useful for all emergency services ; the U.S. police and army forces have adopted it already[1]. The audience shows enthusiasm and great interest which spurred the radio industry on to the manufacture of FM receivers on a large scale. The circle of those who benefit from this invention is ever widening—in December 1941 there were 180,000 FM sets (as compared with 15,000 at the beginning of the year). The broadcasters of other continents are prevented from following in this path only because of the lack of financial means and raw materials and also perhaps for fear of a complete upheaval in the industry. A British expert, E.P. Butt, even suggests[2] that, after the war, the European radio should definitely give up long and medium waves and replace them by ultra-short waves[3]. This bold suggestion is based on the consideration

---

[1] The inventor has offered the free use of his 17 basic FM patents for national defence purposes in the present emergency ; the army is acquiring a large number of FM receivers and developing three new radio sets in which FM will be incorporated for the use of the armoured forces. See *Broadcasting*, March 24, 1941.

[2] *Wireless World*, London, November 1941.

[3] Since January 1942 the Danish broadcasting service has made experimental FM transmissions.

that the use of ultra-high frequencies would make it possible to cover every national territory with a great number of stations, each ensuring a perfect service within a determined area, undisturbed by foreign stations. As for international broadcasting, it could continue to use short waves, as it does today.

Another amazing technical device is the Facsimile Service—the broadcasting of printed matter. It is really a new method of photo-telegraphy, using short waves instead of telephone lines for the transmission of recorded images. Highly perfected, it permits the transmission of newspapers in their entirety, with an average reproduction rate of 350 words a minute ; a news bulletin which takes a quarter of an hour to read over the microphone, may thus be broadcast in a few minutes. In the United States, which alone have such a service at present, there are already some twenty experimental stations, and a network of Facsimile stations to cover the whole country is being considered. (The introduction of Frequency Modulation also favours the Facsimile Service ; for in the future it will be possible to transmit and receive simultaneously with the same apparatus printed material and sound broadcasting). It is not however certain what the future reserves for this invention, whether Facsimile will be developed mainly as a business service or as a service for the general public ; for if Facsimile is of great importance for the business world and especially for provincial newspapers, the general public has not yet accepted it.

Of all these inventions, Television is certainly the most promising and excites the greatest interests and hopes, notwithstanding certain disappointments caused by experiments which were either unsuccessful or undertaken with inadequate financial means. If there can be no question of television being introduced generally and in all countries for a long time, yet all those who witnessed the instantaneous transmissions in London of national or sporting events know that the future belongs to this new technical "conquest". For it is fascinating to be able to live "history in the making" and follow in one's own home the course of a tennis match or the Derby. The main function of television will always be information, including many outside pickups ; it will be moreover an excellent means of education, adding the visual to the sound effect, and a remarkable entertainment able to offer spectacular programmes such as plays, ballets or fashion parades. The analysis of the NBC's first eight months programmes is highly significant ; 33.4% of the total time was reserved for news, special events and sports (transmitted chiefly from outside the studio), 29.1% for drama, 17% for educational programmes (chiefly from films), 11,9% for variety shows, but only 3.5% for music [1]. The effectiveness of television will be further increased by transmission in natural colours, the first showing of which in London and in New York were already fairly promising.

But there are many serious obstacles in the way of the extension of the service. Technical difficulties first, due especially to the limited range of the ultra-short waves—which require numerous stations to cover a wide area—, to the need of separate channels for sound and vision, and of standards for transmission and reception ; another obstacle is the small size of the picture on the receiving screen. Even more serious are the financial difficulties : the enormous cost of installation and running, but also the prohibitive price of receivers.

Certain technical problems have already been partially solved, in the United States at least, by the building of numerous stations, the adoption of standards [2]—525 scanning lines and 30 pictures per second—the use of FM for sound transmission, the use of larger cathode-ray tubes serving as screen (of $7\frac{1}{2}$ x 10 inches in general) and the development of projection on a large screen (15 by 20 feet) for public demonstrations. But the financial obstacles still remain, a 30 by 50 feet television studio equipped for three cameras involving (according to the declaration of the director of the NBC Television Service) an expenditure of $120,000 ; each mobile unit for outside pickups costs $40,000, a projector for film trans-

---

[1] *Cf.* David Sarnoff "Possible Social Effects of Television" in *The Annals*, January 1941, p. 148.

[2] *Cf.* New Rules and Regulations Governing Commercial Television Broadcast Stations, promulgated by the FCC, Washington April 30, 1941 (Effective July 1, 1941).

mission $10,000, and one hourly programme from a big station needs an average of $971,50 ; and the price of receivers is still 150-395 dollars [1].

But notwithstanding these hindrances, many broadcasting companies have begun to work on television, especially in the United States, where there are already 34 experimental and 8 commercial stations, some of 15 and 30 kW. The most important video transmitters belonging to the NBC, the CBS, and the General Electric Co. provide a regular service of at least fifteen hours a week [2]. So far 15 to 20 million dollars have been spent on the development of television, on the stations and programmes [3] ; commercial advertising, allowed only since July 1, 1941 and still necessarily limited, will not be able to cover that expenditure.

In Europe, the BBC—a pioneer in this field—operated an important station in London and enjoyed the best developed service ; but it was suspended at the outbreak of the war. The same occurred in France, where a 30 kW transmitter worked at the Paris Eiffel Tower, in Italy and Soviet Russia. The German radio alone continues its experimental transmissions, but the reception of them is limited to a few public projection premises. Experiments have also been made in Japan and in the Argentine. The number of 'viewers' is still very limited ; they were estimated at 15,000 in London and 7,000 only in the United States. But like radio broadcasting, television will develop collective reception. 600 of the receivers in New York are in public places. The number of theatres and cinemas equipped for the reception of television programmes will increase rapidly, since telecasts have an attraction equal to that of the best films. Television is also used today

---

[1] Herman S. Hettinger "Organizing Radio's Discoveries for Use", in *The Annals*, January 1941, p. 175.

[2] Certain television programmes of the NBC station in New York are picked up directly and rebroadcast by the station of the General Electric Co. in Schenectady and transmitted via the ultra-high-frequency radio relay system to the station of the Philco Corporation in Phidelphia. Once the new DuMont transmitter in Washington is completed, the four companies will form the first television network, linking the stations in these four cities.

[3] Hettinger in the study quoted above, p. 182.

for national defence : soon after the entry into the war of the U.S.A., the television services, in cooperation with the American Television Society, arranged programmes for the training of the New York City air raid wardens and Red Cross workers ; after a few weeks, the Chairman of the FCC stated that these civilian defence courses reached more than 50,000 people in the New York area.

Some people had thought that television would prove to be the mortal enemy of broadcasting—but the contrary is true for the addition of vision to sound broadcasting is similar to the addition of sound to the silent film. It is in *adding* to broadcasting that television will find its greatest possibilities and its greatest successes. However, "the road of application is long", as an American expert has said [1]. But manufacturers believe "in the future of television, which will carry radio broadcasting far beyong its present state of development" [2].

The general application of these new discoveries—FM, Facsimile and Television—could greatly enrich our minds. But their role and their value depend entirely on the use to which they will be put ; like all technical inventions, and indeed, like radio broadcasting, they can be used for "good or for evil".

------

[1] Herman S. Hettinger, in the study quoted above, p. 181.

[2] This expression of belief is to be found in a letter of the Radio Corporation of America (RCA), accompanying the NBC applications for new television stations. *Cf. Broadcasting*, June 23, 1941, p. 54.

THE MOST POWERFUL STATIONS IN THE WORLD

A. Long and medium-wave stations

Power in kW	Station	Country
500	Moscow-Komintern (RW 1) . . .	U.S.S.R.
450	Radio-Paris (Allouis)	France
200	Radio-Luxembourg	Luxemburg
180	Villa Acuña XERA [1]	Mexico
150	Lahti [2]	Finland
	Deutschlandsender (Herzberg) . .	Germany
	Droitwich National	Great Britain
	Radio-Romania (Brasov)	Rumania
	Motala	Sweden
	Mexico City XEDP[3]	Mexico
	Monterrey XEG [4]	
	Tokyo I	Japan
	Tokyo II	—
135	Buenos Aires LR 3 (Radio Belgrano)	Argentina
125	Hilversum I (Lopik)	Netherlands
	Hilversum II (Lopik)	—
120	Prague I (Liblitz)	Bohemia and Moravia
	Paris PTT [5]	France
	Rennes-Bretagne	—
	Toulouse-Pyrénées	—
	Leipzig	Germany
	Vienna-Bisamberg	— (Östmark)
	Warsaw I-Raszyn [6]	Poland Gen. Gov.
	Kootwijk [7]	Netherlands
	Budapest I	Hungary
	Ankara TAR	Turkey

[1] Closed June 9, 1941 by order of the Mexican Government.
[2] Original power 220 kW, reduced in 1941.
[3] Operating power 50 kW (Sept. 1941).
[4] Operating power 500 Watts (Sept. 1941).
[5] Destroyed during military operations but is being rebuilt.
[6] Now operated by Germany under the name of "Weichsel".
[7] Now operated by Germany under the name of "Friesland".

Power in kW.	Station	Country
100	Dobrochau	Bohemia and Moravia
	Radio-Sofia	Bulgaria
	Zagreb [1]	Croatia
	Athlone	Eire (Ireland)
	Lyon PTT (La Doua)	France
	Marseille PTT	—
	« Alpen »	Germany
	Berlin	—
	Bremen	—
	Breslau	—
	Hamburg	—
	Koenigsberg I (Heilsberg) . . .	—
	Koeln (Langenberg)	—
	Munich	—
	Stuttgart (Müblacker)	—
	Lisnagarvey (Northern Ireland Regional)	Great Britain
	Start Point	—
	Reykjavik	Iceland
	Florence I	Italy
	Rome I	—
	Vigra [2]	Norway
	Stavanger	—
	Bucarest [3]	Rumania
	Bratislava I [1]	Slovakia
	Falun	Sweden
	Beromünster	Switzerland
	Sottens	—
	Brovary RW87	U.S.S.R.
	Leningrad-Kolpino	—
	Moscow RW39	—
	Moscow RW43	—
	Moscow RW49	—
	Novosibirsk RW46	—
	Buenos Aires LR 4 (Radio Splendid) [1]	Argentina
	Mexico City XEW	Mexico
	Mexico City XEB [4]	—
	Reynosa XEAW	—
	Kiushu [1]	Japan
	Osaka [1]	—
	Hsingking II	Manchukuo

[1] Under construction.
[2] Power reduced to 1 kW.
[3] Planned.
[4] Operating power 20 kW (Sept. 1941).

B. SHORT-WAVE STATIONS [1]

Power in kW.	Station	Country
100	Paris-Mondial (Allouis)	France
	Daventry (Overseas Transmitters)	Great Britain
	Prato Smeraldo (Rome)	Italy
	Moscow RW96	U.S.S.R.
	Bound Brook WRCA [2]	U.S.A.
	Schenectady WGEO	—
	San Francisco KWID [3]	—
	Scituate, Mass. WRUS [3].	—
80	Kootwijk PCV	Netherlands
75	Mason, Ohio WLWO	U.S.A.
60	Huizen PCJ	Netherlands
50	Zeesen (Deutscher Kurzwellensender)	Germany
	Daventry (Overseas Transmitters)	Great Britain
	Prato Smeraldo (Rome)	Italy
	Lisbon [3]	Portugal
	Moscow	U.S.S.R.
	Belmont, Cal. KGGI	U.S.A.
	Bound Brook WNBI	—
	Brentwood WCRC	—
	Brentwood WCBX	—
	Hull, Mass. WBOS	—
	Schenectady WGEA	—
	Scituate, Mass. WRUW and WRUL	—
	Buenos Aires [3]	Argentina
	Rio de Janeiro PRE8 [3]	Brazil
	Tokyo	Japan
35	Chungking XGOX and XGOY . .	China
30	Podiebrad	Bohemia and Moravia
	Caracas YVKB and YVSC	Venezuela
	Maracay YVQ	—
25	Paris-Mondial (Les Essarts le Roi)	France
	Prato Smeraldo (Rome)	Italy
	Schwarzenburg.	Switzerland
	Radio-Vaticana	Vatican City
	Buenos Aires LRX [3]	Argentina
	Port-au-Prince [4]	Haiti

[1] Different stations have two and more transmitters each.
[2] Operates also with 50 kW.
[3] Under construction.
[4] Not in operation since 1937.

NUMBER AND DENSITY OF RADIO HOMES *

(January 1, 1941)

Number		Density per 1000 inhabitants	
U.S.A.	29.397.000 [1]	Sweden.	231.87
Germany	14.965.048	Denmark	225.43
U.S.S.R. [2] . . .	10.551.361	U.S.A.	223.26
Great Britain [3] . .	9.132.200	New Zealand . . .	212.10
Japan	5.369.898	Great Britain [3] . . .	197.70
France	5.133.035	Australia	173.30
China [4]	2.000.000	Germany	166.27
Canada	1.676.530	Netherlands . . .	163.07
Sweden.	1.470.375	Switzerland	151.81
Netherlands. . .	1.440.626	Iceland [9]	150.48
Italy	1.400.000	Canada	148.15
Australia [5] . . .	1.212.581	Norway	145.46
Belgium [6]	1.148.659	Belgium [6]	136.96
Poland [7] . . .	1.021.874	Luxemburg [10] . . .	122.59
Argentina [4] . . .	1.000.000	France	122.50
Denmark	863.400	Bohemia-Moravia .	114.14
Bohemia-Moravia	840.085	Finland.	89.63
Switzerland . . .	637.612	Japan	77.54
Hungary	609.868	Argentina.	76.16
Mexico [4]	450.000	Uruguay	70.65
Norway	429.412	U.S.S.R. [2]	62.07
New Zealand . .	352.055	Eire (Ireland) . . .	60.54
Brazil	376.510	Hungary	45.20
Finland.	348.483	Venezuela [8]	38.17
Union of S. Africa	283.119	Cuba	35.27
Spain	281.430	Chile	32.02
Rumania	244.309	Slovakia [11]	31.28
Eire (Ireland) . .	179.563	Italy	31.11
Jugoslavia [8] . . .	177.405	Palestine [12]	31.05
Chile [4]	150.000	Poland [7]	29.59
Cuba [4]	150.000	Union of S. Africa .	29.52
Uruguay [4]. . . .	150.000	Mexico	23.42
Venezuela [8] . . .	138.000	Rumania	19.23
India	119.417	Algeria	14.83
Algeria	107.312	Portugal [13]	14.36
Dutch East Indies	100.347	Spain	11.94
Colombia [4] . . .	100.000	Colombia	11.36

[1] Total number of sets : 52,000,000. [2] Sept. 30, 1940. [3] June 30, 1940. [4] Estimation. [5] June 30, 1940. [6] January 1, 1940. [7] July 31, 1940. [8] Automne 1940. [9] Number of sets 18,261. [10] January 1, 1940, number of sets 36,954. [11] 83,024 sets. [12] 46,629 sets, July 31, 1940. [13] 98,030 sets.
* Sources : Diagrams and information of the International Broadcasting Office, Geneva ; documents of the Federal Communications Commission and the U. S. Department of Commerce, Washington ; *Broadcasting*, Yearbook 1941.

DEVELOPMENT OF RADIO AND PRESS
(FCC EXHIBIT IX)

Number of US Broadcast Stations and Receiving Sets compared with
Number of Newspapers and their Circulation: 1922-40 *

Year	Number of Stations	Total Radio Sets in Use [1]	Number of Daily Newspapers	Total Circulation of Daily Newspapers
1922 (1. I.) . . .	30	400.000	2.033	29.680.328
1923 (1. III.) . .	556	1.500.000	2.036	31.453.683
1924 (1. X.) . . .	530	3.000.000	2.005	32.999.437
1925 (30. VI.) . .	571	4.000.000	2.008	33.739.369
1926 (30. VI.) . .	528	5.000.000	2.001	36.001.803
1927 (23. II.) . .	733	6.500.000	1.949	37.966.766
1928 (1. VII) . .	677	8.500.000	1.939	37.972.592
1929 (9. XI.) . .	618	10.500.000	1.944	39.425.615
1930 (1. VII.) . .	612	13.000.000	1.942	39.589.172
1931 (1. VII.) . .	612	15.000.000	1.923	38.761.187
1932 (1. I.) . . .	608	18.000.000	1.913	36.407.297
1933 (1. I.) . . .	610	22.000.000	1.911	35.175.238
1934 (1. I.) . . .	591	28.000.000	1.929	36.709.010
1935 (1. I.) . . .	605	30.500.000	1.950	38.155.540
1936 (1. I.) . . .	632	33.000.000	1.989	40.292.266
1937 (1. I.) . . .	685	37.600.000	1.983	41.418.730
1938 (1. I.) . . .	721	40.800.000	1.936	39.571.839
1939 (1. I.) . . .	764	45.200.000	1.888	39.670.682
1940 (1. I.) . . .	814	50.100.000	1.877	41.009.258

[1] These figures include auto-sets, portable sets and additional sets in use in homes. The number of auto-sets advanced from 100,000 in 1931 to 3,500,000 in 1936 to 9,300,000 in 1941.

* Sources: Number of Broadcast Stations, Records of FCC. Total Radio Sets in Use, Estimates by O.H. Caldwell, editor of *Radio Retailing Today*. Number of Daily Newspapers and Total Circulation of Daily Newspapers, *Editor & Publisher* Yearbooks.

SELECTED BIBLIOGRAPHY [1]

Publications of the broadcasting services : reports, annuals, handbooks and official magazines.

Monthly bulletins and diagrams of the International Broadcasting Union, Geneva.

Lists of Broadcasting Stations and documents of international radio-communication conferences, published by the Bureau of the International Telecommunication Union.

Journal des Télécommunications, Berne (official organ of the Bureau of the International Telecommunication Union).

Reports, documents and statistics of the Federal Communications Commission, Washington D.C.

Radio, Telephone, Telegraph (formerly *World Radio Markets*), issued by the U.S. Department of Commerce, Electrical Division, Washington D.C.

Broadcasting (Weekly), Washington D.C., and its Yearbook-Numbers 1940 and 1941.

Radio Daily, New York.

Variety (Weekly), New York.

Wireless World (Monthly), London.

Antena (Weekly), Buenos Aires.

Rundfunkarchiv (Monthly), Berlin.

Weltrundfunk, Heidelberg.

Handbuch des Deutschen Rundfunks, edited by H.J. Weinbrenner, Heidelberg, 1938/39 and 1939/40.

"New Horizons in Radio", special number of *The Annals*, edited by Herman S. Hettinger, Philadelphia, Jan. 1941.

---

[1] For want of space a more extensive bibliography could not be included. The reader is referred to the footnotes.

HISTORY OF BROADCASTING:
Radio To Television
An Arno Press/New York Times Collection

Archer, Gleason L.
Big Business and Radio. 1939.

Archer, Gleason L.
History of Radio to 1926. 1938.

Arnheim, Rudolf.
Radio. 1936.

Blacklisting: Two Key Documents. 1952–1956.

Cantril, Hadley and Gordon W. Allport.
The Psychology of Radio. 1935.

Codel, Martin, editor.
Radio and Its Future. 1930.

Cooper, Isabella M.
Bibliography on Educational Broadcasting. 1942.

Dinsdale, Alfred.
First Principles of Television. 1932.

Dunlap, Orrin E., Jr.
Marconi: The Man and His Wireless. 1938.

Dunlap, Orrin E., Jr.
The Outlook for Television. 1932.

Fahie, J. J.
A History of Wireless Telegraphy. 1901.

Federal Communications Commission.
Annual Reports of the Federal Communications Commission.
1934/1935–1955.

Federal Radio Commission.
Annual Reports of the Federal Radio Commission. 1927–1933.

Frost, S. E., Jr.
Education's Own Stations. 1937.

Grandin, Thomas.
The Political Use of the Radio. 1939.

Harlow, Alvin.
Old Wires and New Waves. 1936.

Hettinger, Herman S.
A Decade of Radio Advertising. 1933.

Huth, Arno.
Radio Today: The Present State of Broadcasting. 1942.

Jome, Hiram L.
Economics of the Radio Industry. 1925.

Lazarsfeld, Paul F.
Radio and the Printed Page. 1940.

Lumley, Frederick H.
Measurement in Radio. 1934.

Maclaurin, W. Rupert.
Invention and Innovation in the Radio Industry. 1949.

Radio: Selected A.A.P.S.S. Surveys. 1929–1941.

Rose, Cornelia B., Jr.
National Policy for Radio Broadcasting. 1940.

Rothafel, Samuel L. and Raymond Francis Yates.
Broadcasting: Its New Day. 1925.

Schubert, Paul.
The Electric Word: The Rise of Radio. 1928.

Studies in the Control of Radio: Nos. 1–6. 1940–1948.

Summers, Harrison B., editor.
Radio Censorship. 1939.

Summers, Harrison B., editor.
A Thirty-Year History of Programs Carried on National Radio Networks in the United States, 1926–1956. 1958.

Waldrop, Frank C. and Joseph Borkin.
Television: A Struggle for Power. 1938.

White, Llewellyn.
The American Radio. 1947.

World Broadcast Advertising: Four Reports. 1930–1932.